# Campground Cooking

## Over 200 Fun & Easy Recipes For Your RV or Grill
## ...or easy cooking at home

## By Patricia Watson

I

ISBN#0-9740565-0-2

## Publication #9036

*Printed in the United States of America by:*

**G & R Publishing Company**
507 Industrial Street
Waverly, IA  50677
800-383-1679
gandr@gandrpublishing.com
http://www.cookbookprinting.com

This book is dedicated to a very special person....
my friend, Dixie Hendricks,
whose love and support made this book possible.

*Some people come into our lives,*
*and quickly go.........*
*Others stay for awhile,*
*and leave a footprint on our hearts.*

Author Unknown

# KOA Care Camps
HAPPINESS FOR KIDS WITH CANCER

Having cancer shouldn't mean giving up the joys of childhood. That's why the KOA Kampground Owners Association created the Care Camps Trust—to help children who have cancer enjoy care-free time focusing on fun, friends and activities at sleep-away camp instead of on their illness.

The Care Camps Trust provides financial support to 37 special nonprofit camps located throughout the United States and Canada. These facilities are fully-equipped with the necessary medical supplies and volunteer professional staff to care for campers' cancer-related needs.

Your gift to KOA Care Camps will help provide the opportunity for a greater number of special children to enjoy camping experiences and help them to remember what it's like to "just be a kid."

Beginning in 1984, the KOA Care Camps Trust began donating to children's cancer camps being developed in many areas of the United States and Canada which offered tremendous benefits for children living with cancer. The $7,100 that KOA owners and their campers donated during the first year of the program supported six camps in the United States. Since 1984, the program has grown to include a total of 37 camps in the United States and Canada. Approximately two camps are added each year. Last year, KOA donated $200,000 to support the camps. Even though staff members volunteer their time and services, expenses for these programs are still quite substantial. Costs include medications, medical equipment, utilities, insurance, and transportation, plus those for camping program basics such as meals and recreation equipment.

Your gift, regardless of size, will help these special programs to serve the children who need them. Donations may be made in honor or memory of a loved one, and all donations will be acknowledged.

Please send your donation or request for additional information to:

**KOA Care Camps**
**3416 Primm Lane, P.O. Box 361064**
**Birmingham, Alabama 35236-1064**
**E-mail: Info@koaowners.org**

KOA CARE CAMPS IS A TRUST CREATED BY
THE KOA KAMPGROUND OWNERS ASSOCIATION

**10% OF THE AUTHOR'S PROFITS FROM THIS BOOK WILL GO TO THE KOA CARE CAMPS TRUST. ON BEHALF OF THE CHILDREN AND KOA, THE AUTHOR THANKS YOU FOR YOUR SUPPORT.**

# WITH SINCERE APPRECIATION....

Saying thank you just does not seem like enough to my editor, Dolores Sobczak, who spent much time helping me put this cookbook together. Thank you so much, Dolores, for your support and enthusiasm!

To all of my very special friends at the great Holland American Legion Post #646.....Wendy Mayberry, I thank you so much for the hours and the headaches it took to help me proofread this book. Thank you, Katie Roop, for your expertise (and tremendous patience) assisting me where my computer skills were lacking. To Jill Boulton, Kelly Reed, and many, many more (too numerous to mention), I thank you from the bottom of my heart for all of your support. You tolerated my constant talking about "food"; you were always willing to try my new recipes; and you contributed many ideas for use in this book. I am truly grateful, and every one of you will always have a special place in my heart.

To my wonderful friends at the KOA Big Sandy Campground in Swanton, Ohio.....Terri Hughes and again, friends too numerous to mention, I thank you all for your support and encouragement. Looking forward to many more years of fun, and of course cooking, with all of you!

To the staff at G & R Publishing.....a sincere thank you for all of your guidance in the typesetting and printing of this book. Your patience and friendliness is greatly appreciated.

To my fantastic family.....my daughters, Lori, Mollie, and Leslie, my son and daughter-in-law, Mike and Tina, all of my grandchildren, and my siblings, I thank you for your constant love and support.

To my special friend, David Hendricks.....thank you for spending many hours sitting at the campground reading cookbooks with me and helping me come up with new ideas for recipes. What a guy!

I have saved the best for last.....my husband, Francis Watson. How do I find the words to thank you for all you have done for me? I will always be forever thankful—your love and support has truly made this book a reality. I feel blessed for having such a wonderful husband as you, and I will always be grateful. Thanks, Fran!

# FROM THE AUTHOR....

Campers are very special people. They come from all walks of life, and head to the campground for some fun and relaxation—whether it be for a weekend, a week, or a month. The stresses of everyday life are left far behind. Walking around a campground compares to taking a stroll through a small town—everyone is friendly and there are no strangers.

Campers love to cook. This book is designed to make cooking at the campground fun and easy—with minimal cleanup tasks. As you will see in my book, most recipes are made in a 9x9" pan, which will fit in most camper ovens. Stoneware, sprayed with nonstick cooking spray, works well for these recipes and makes cleanup quick and easy. For most salads and desserts, I recommend using an 8x8" or 9x9" square plastic container, which fits well in camper refrigerators.

Camper refrigerators are usually small—use your creativity to save precious space. Whole onions and green peppers can be cleaned and cut, and stored in plastic sealable bags. Eggs can be slightly beaten, put in ice cube trays to freeze, then stored in the freezer in plastic sealable bags.

Plan to let a good fire burn at least 15 to 20 minutes to provide enough coals for cooking. You should be able to hold your hand about 4 inches above the coals, having to pull away after 4 seconds. When cooking outside with an electric skillet, put a small piece of paneling on the picnic table, under the skillet, to protect plastic tablecloths. This piece of paneling doubles as extra counter space when put on top of your stove in the camper.

Plan ahead for leftovers and save on your food bill. Leftover hamburgers will make a pot of "Hamburger Dump Stew"; leftover hot dogs are great for "Saucy Dogs"; save leftover bacon to put on "BBQ Bacon Cheeseburgers"; or cut up leftover chicken for "Hot Chicken Salad." Leftover potatoes from dinner can easily be reheated for breakfast the next morning.

You don't have to be a camper to enjoy my book. This book is filled with fun, easy recipes that can also be made at home. Most recipes can be doubled for larger families and cooked in a 9x13" pan. Whether you are a camper or a busy mom, this cookbook is for you!

# CONTENTS

## APPETIZERS, SNACKS AND DIPS

## BREAKFAST

### GRILL

### MICROWAVE

### OVEN

### SKILLET

## TOASTER

## WAFFLE IRON

# MAIN DISHES AND CASSEROLES

## CROCK POT

## COVERED GRILL

## MICROWAVE

## OVEN

## SKILLET

## STOVETOP

# MEAT, POULTRY AND SEAFOOD

## CROCK POT

## GRILL

## OVEN

## SKILLET

## STOVETOP

# FOIL COOKING

# SOUPS, SALADS AND SANDWICHES

# VEGETABLES AND SIDE DISHES

## CROCK POT

## MICROWAVE

## OVEN

## REFRIGERATOR

## SKILLET

# DESSERTS

# MISCELLANEOUS

# APPETIZERS

# My Favorites

## BBQ WATERCHESTNUTS

Page 13

2-8 oz. cans whole waterchestnuts
1 C. ketchup
1 lb. bacon
1 C. sugar

Cut raw bacon in half. Wrap waterchestnuts in bacon, using 1/2 piece of bacon for each waterchestnut. Secure each with a toothpick and place on a cookie sheet or shallow baking pan (use a pan with edges to prevent (grease from running off). Bake at 350 degrees for 1 hour. **(Complete Recipe on Page 13)**

## SUSIE'S SHRIMP DIP

Page 12

1-4 oz. can tiny shrimp, drained
1/2 C. celery, finely chopped
1/4 C. onion, finely chopped

1/2 C. mayonnaise
Pepper
Crackers

In a bowl, combine shrimp, celery, onion, and mayonnaise. Season as desired with pepper. Serve with crackers. **(Recipe on Page 12)**

## SNACKER CRACKERS

1-14 oz. pkg. oyster crackers
1-1 oz. env. Ranch dressing
  mix
Pinch of salt

3/4 C. vegetable oil
1/4 tsp. garlic powder

Heat oil with seasonings. Put crackers in a large heavy-duty brown paper bag. Pour seasoned oil quickly over crackers. Shake well. Cool and store in an airtight container or storage bag.

## PUPPY CHOW

1 stick butter, softened
1 C. chocolate chips
1/2 C. peanut butter

1-13 oz. box toasted corn cereal
2 C. powdered sugar

Mix butter, chocolate chips, and peanut butter in a 1-qt. microwave-safe bowl. Cook on high for about 2 minutes, or until melted. Put cereal in a large bowl, pour chocolate chip mixture over cereal. Stir, or cover and shake, until well coated. Transfer mixture to another bowl with powdered sugar in it. Cover and shake well to coat. Enjoy!

## CUCUMBER MIX

2 cucumbers
1-8 oz. pkg. cream cheese
Cocktail rye bread

1 C. mayonnaise
1-1 oz. pkg. Ranch dressing mix
Finely chopped onions, if desired

Finely chop peeled cucumbers. Mix cucumbers with cream cheese, mayonnaise, Ranch dressing mix, and onions. Spread on slices of cocktail rye bread and serve.

## NACHO CHEESE DIP

1 lb. ground beef
Nacho chips

2-10 3/4 oz. cans nacho cheese soup

Brown ground beef and drain. Add nacho cheese soup and mix well. Heat until warm. Serve with nacho chips.

# STUFFED WON-TON STARS

**1-1 oz. pkg. Ranch dressing mix**
**1 C. real mayonnaise**
**1 C. sour cream**
**1 lb. hot and spicy bulk**
**sausage**
**1-16 oz. pkg. won-ton wrappers**
**(found in most produce depts.)**

**1-2 1/4 oz. can sliced black olives**
**1 bunch green onions, sliced**
**Diced red pepper (to color)**
**3 C. Cheddar cheese, shredded**

Mix pkg. of Ranch dressing mix, real mayonnaise, and sour cream. Let sit for 1 hour. Meanwhile, lightly spray muffin pans with nonstick cooking spray (first time only is necessary). Line muffin tins with won-ton wrappers and bake at 375 degrees for 5 to 7 minutes or until lightly brown. Turn upside down on paper towels to cool. Brown sausage and drain very well on paper towels. Mix sausage, black olives (drained), green onions, red pepper, cheese, and mayonnaise mixture. Stuff cooled won-ton wrappers with filling and bake at 375 degrees for an additional 5 to 7 minutes or until cheese melts.

Baked won-ton wrappers can also be used with numerous fillings without additional baking. Try refried beans topped with salsa, cheese, and sour cream; or try chocolate pudding topped with whipped cream and nuts. Be creative!

# GARLIC CHIVE DIP

**16 oz. sour cream**
**1/2 tsp. minced garlic**
**1 tsp. lemon juice**

**1 T. chopped chives**
**Salt and pepper to taste**

Combine all ingredients and refrigerate for at least 1 hour. Serve with crackers or raw vegetables.

# SUSIE'S SHRIMP DIP

**1-4 oz. can tiny shrimp, drained**
**1/2 C. celery, finely chopped**
**1/4 C. onion, finely chopped**

**1/2 C. mayonnaise**
**Pepper**
**Crackers**

In a bowl, combine shrimp, celery, onion, and mayonnaise. Season as desired with pepper. Serve with crackers.

## VEGETABLE DILL DIP

2 C. real mayonnaise
3 T. dried parsley
1 T. dill weed
1 T. flavor enhancer (Accent)
2 C. sour cream

3 T. minced onion
1 T. seasoned salt
4 1/2 tsp. Worcestershire sauce
5 drops Tabasco sauce

Mix all ingredients together and let sit overnight. Store in an air-tight container. Serve with raw vegetables.

## SPINACH DIP

1-10 oz. frozen chopped
   spinach, thawed and squeezed
   dry
16 oz. sour cream
1 C. real mayonnaise
3 green onions, chopped

1-1.4 oz. pkg. vegetable soup,
   dip, and recipe mix
1-8 oz. can waterchestnuts,
   drained and chopped

Combine all ingredients; chill at least 2 to 3 hours. Serve with your choice of crackers, cubed or cocktail rye bread. May be served in a bread bowl, if desired.

## BBQ WATERCHESTNUTS

2-8 oz. cans whole
   waterchestnuts
1 lb. bacon

1 C. ketchup
1 C. sugar

Cut raw bacon in half. Wrap waterchestnuts in bacon, using 1/2 piece of bacon for each waterchestnut. Secure each with a toothpick and place on a cookie sheet or shallow baking pan (use a pan with edges to prevent grease from running off). Bake at 350 degrees for 1 hour. Combine ketchup and sugar; heat in a skillet. Place waterchestnuts in ketchup mixture and simmer for 5 minutes. Serve with ketchup mixture as a dipping sauce.

# MINI REUBEN SANDWICHES

**Cocktail rye bread**
**Deli corned beef, sliced thin**
**Sauerkraut, drained well**
   **dressing**

**Swiss cheese slices**
**Thousand Island salad**

Spread half of the rye bread slices out on a cookie sheet. Layer each slice with corned beef, sauerkraut, Swiss cheese, and salad dressing. Top each with another slice of rye bread. Bake at 350 degrees about 10 minutes or until light browned and cheese is melted.

TIP: When making this recipe, be sure to make plenty since these little sandwiches go quickly!

# AVOCADO DIP

**2 avocados**
**1-8 oz. pkg. cream cheese,**
   **softened**

**1 T. onion, finely chopped**
**1/2 tsp. garlic salt**

Mash peeled avocados in a mixing bowl. Add remaining ingredients and mix at medium speed with mixer until well blended. Serve with crackers or tortilla chips.

# PARTY NUTS

**2 C. whole almonds, peanuts,**
   **cashews or mixed nuts**
**3 T. butter or margarine**

**1 tsp. celery salt**
**1/2 tsp. chili powder**
**1/8 tsp. ground red pepper**

In a skillet, sauté nuts in butter over low heat until golden, about 5 minutes. Drain off excess butter. In a bowl, combine celery salt, chili powder, and red pepper. Toss the nuts with the spice mixture until well coated. Spread nuts out on foil to cool.

MICROWAVE METHOD: Combine butter, celery salt, chili powder, and red pepper in a microwave-safe bowl. Cook, uncovered, on high for 40 to 50 seconds, until butter is melted. Stir in nuts. Cook, uncovered, for 6 to 7 minutes or until nuts are toasted, stirring every 2 minutes for the first 4 minutes, then every 30 seconds. Spread on foil to cool.

## MUSHROOM NIBBLERS

**Canned whole mushrooms**          **Caesar salad dressing**

Drain mushrooms.  Cover mushrooms with salad dressing; cover and store in refrigerator for 3 to 4 hours.  Drain and serve with toothpicks.

## SALMON DIP

**1-14 oz. can red salmon, drained**          **1/2 tsp. onion powder**
**   flaked, and skin and bones**                 **1/2 tsp. celery seed**
**   removed**                                            **1/8 tsp. pepper**
**2 stalks celery, finely chopped**               **Crackers**
**1/2 C. mayonnaise**
**1 T. lemon juice**

In a bowl, combine the salmon, celery, mayonnaise, lemon juice, onion powder, celery seed and pepper.  Cover and chill until ready to serve.  Serve with crackers.

If desired, an additional 1 to 2 T. of mayonnaise can be added for a creamier texture.  Garnish top with sliced black olives, if desired.

# CHICKEN QUESADILLAS

2 C. Mexican-flavored cheese,
  shredded
6 flour tortillas (8-10")
1 C. chicken, cooked and
  chopped

1 small tomato, chopped
4 green onions, chopped
2 T. chopped green chilies
Salsa and sour cream

Sprinkle 1/3 C. of cheese evenly over half of each tortilla. Sprinkle remaining ingredients over cheese. Fold tortillas in half over filling. Place on a cookie sheet and bake at 350 degrees for about 5 minutes, or just until cheese is melted. Serve whole or cut into wedges, with salsa and sour cream if desired.

TIP: If cutting quesadillas into wedges, begin cutting from the center of folded side of tortillas.

---

# NOTES:

# BREAKFAST

# My Favorites

## PIEROGIES BREAKFAST

8 oz. frozen potato pierogies
(about 6 pierogies)
1/2 lb. bacon
4 eggs, beaten

1/2 C. Cheddar cheese, shredded
1/2 C. onion, chopped
1/2 C. green pepper, chopped

Fry bacon in skillet until browned.  Drain on paper towels, reserving 1 T. of the fat.  Break bacon into 1/2" pieces and set aside.  Thaw **(Complete Recipe on page 24)**

## EGG PIE
Page 22

6 eggs
1/3 C. milk
1/2 sm. onion, chopped
1/2 sm. green pepper, chopped
1 unbaked pie crust

1-4 oz. can sliced mushrooms
1 C. ham chunks (8 oz.)
1/2 C. Cheddar cheese, shredded

Combine eggs and milk in a bowl.  Add onions, green pepper, mushrooms, ham, and cheese.  Mix well and pour into unbaked pie crust. Bake at 350 degrees for 40 to 50 minutes or until eggs are set.  Set sit for 5 minutes.  Serve with salsa if desired.  **(Recipe on page 22)**

# CROCK POT

## CAMPER DAVE'S EGG CASSEROLE
(oven, microwave, or grill)

4 eggs, beaten
1/2 tsp. salt
3 slices of bread
1/2 tsp. dry mustard
1 C. milk
1/2 C. ham, cubed
1/2 small onion, chopped
1/2 C. Cheddar cheese, shredded
1/2 small green pepper, chopped

Cut bread into bite-size cubes. Mix all ingredients together and store in refrigerator overnight in a covered bowl. Next day, pour into a 9x9" pan, sprayed with nonstick cooking spray. Bake 1 hour at 350 degrees. Instead of baking, this recipe can be cooked in a microwave for 25 minutes or in a covered grill on the top rack for 45 minutes.

This recipe is to be prepared the night before, or can be prepared at home and taken to the campground to bake the next morning.

# MICROWAVE

## PIZZA PANCAKES                                    (microwave)

FOR TWO SERVINGS:
| | |
|---|---|
| 4 precooked sausage links | 4 frozen pancakes |
| 3 eggs | 1/4 C. strawberry jam |
| 3 T. milk | 1/2 C. Cheddar cheese, shredded |

In a small microwave-safe bowl, combine eggs and milk; beat well. Cover loosely with plastic wrap and microwave on high for 1 to 2 minutes or until set, stirring once. Place 2 pancakes, side by side, on each of 2 plates. Spread each pancake with strawberry jam and top with cooked eggs, cheese, and sliced sausage. Microwave on high for 1 to 2 minutes or until pancake is thoroughly heated and cheese is melted.

# BACON HASH BROWN CASSEROLE (microwave)

1/2 lb. bacon
3 C. frozen shredded hash
  browns
1/2 small onion, chopped
1/2 small green pepper, chopped
1-4 1/2 oz. can sliced mushrooms,
  drained

1 T. butter
3 eggs
1/8 C. milk
1 C. Cheddar cheese,
  shredded

Fry bacon, cool and crumble, set aside. In a 2-qt microwave-safe dish, combine hash browns, onion, green peppers, mushrooms, and butter. Cover and microwave on high for 6 to 7 minutes or until vegetables are tender, stirring once. Beat eggs and milk; stir into vegetable mixture. Cover and cook at 70% power for 5 to 6 minutes or until eggs are almost set, stirring every 2 minutes. Sprinkle with cheese and bacon. Cook, uncovered, on high for 1 to 2 minutes or until cheese is melted. Let stand 5 minutes before serving.

Frozen hash browns with onions and green peppers can be used in this recipe; use 3 C. of these hash browns and omit chopped onion and green pepper.

# OVEN

## BREAKFAST PIZZA (oven)

1 lb. spicy bulk sausage
1-8 oz. pkg. crescent rolls
3 C. frozen hash browns with
  onions and green peppers

8 oz. mozzarella cheese, shredded
3 eggs, beaten well
1 T. milk
Parmesan cheese

Thaw hash browns (can be done in a microwave). Cook sausage until no longer pink. Drain well on paper towels. Place dough on pizza pan sprayed with nonstick cooking spray. Press dough together to form a solid crust. Pinch up edges of dough. Spread one-half of thawed hash browns on crust. Spread sausage on top of hash browns. Spread remaining one-half of hash browns on top of sausage. Sprinkle mozzarella cheese on top of hash browns. Combine eggs and milk; pour over top of cheese. Sprinkle lightly with Parmesan cheese. Bake at 375 degrees for 25 minutes or until lightly browned. Serve with salsa if desired.

# CHEESY SAUSAGE HASH BROWN CASSEROLE

(oven)

4 C. frozen hash browns with
  onions and green peppers
1 lb. bulk sausage, hot or mild
1 C. Cheddar cheese, shredded

1-10 3/4 oz. can cream of
  chicken soup
1/2 C. sour cream
1/2 C. French onion dip

Thaw hash browns (can be done in the microwave). In a skillet, cook the sausage until browned; drain well. In a bowl, combine the cheese, soup, sour cream, and French onion dip. Fold in thawed hash browns. Mix well. Spread one-half of the hash brown mixture over the bottom of a 9x9" pan, sprayed with nonstick cooking spray. Spread one-half of the sausage over hash browns. Repeat layers, ending with sausage. Bake at 350 degrees for 1 hour or until casserole is golden brown. Sprinkle with additional cheese if desired, and let sit for 5 to 10 minutes.

Great served with a side of fried eggs and toast!

# FRENCH TOAST CASSEROLE

(oven)

1/2 loaf French bread, cut into 1"
  cubes (5 cups)
4 eggs
1 1/2 C. milk

2 tsp. sugar
1/2 tsp. vanilla
Maple syrup (optional)

TOPPING:
1 T. butter
1 1/2 T. sugar

1 tsp. cinnamon

Spray a 9x9" pan with nonstick cooking spray. Place bread cubes in an even layer in pan. In a bowl, beat eggs, milk, 2 tsp. sugar, and vanilla. Pour over bread. Cover and refrigerate for 8 hrs. or overnight. Remove mixture from refrigerator 30 minutes before baking. Dot with butter. Combine 1 1/2 T. sugar and cinnamon; sprinkle over top. Cover and bake at 350 degrees for 45 to 50 minutes or until a knife inserted near the center comes out clean. Let stand for 5 minutes. Serve with maple syrup if desired.

This recipe is to be prepared the night before.

# SAUSAGE EGG PIE

(oven)

1 lb. bulk sausage, cooked &
  drained
1-12 oz. pkg. refrigerated
  crescent rolls
1 1/2 C. mozzarella cheese,
  shredded

2 T. Parmesan cheese
1/4 lb. muenster cheese,
  shredded
4 eggs, beaten

Spray a 9x9" pan with nonstick cooking spray. Line one-half of the pkg. of crescent rolls in bottom of the pan, creating the bottom crust. Spread the cooked sausage evenly over the dough. Top with mozzarella cheese, muenster cheese, and Parmesan cheese. Pour eggs over top. Cover with remaining half of the crescent rolls, creating the top crust. Bake at 350 degrees for 30 minutes or until golden brown.

# MUFFIN-TIN BREAKFAST

(oven)

6 round ham slices, sliced thin
6 eggs

Prepared muffin batter,
  enough to make 6 muffins

Bake breakfast in a nonstick, 12-muffin tin. Line each of 6 tins with a round ham slice. Break an egg into each piece of ham. Salt and pepper eggs, if desired. Line the remaining 6 tins with paper liners. Fill each 2/3 full with muffin batter. Bake at 375 degrees for 15 to 20 minutes or until eggs are desired firmness and muffins are golden brown.

# EGG PIE

(oven)

6 eggs
1/3 C. milk
1/2 sm. onion, chopped
1/2 sm. green pepper, chopped
1 unbaked pie crust

1-4 oz. can sliced mushrooms
1 C. ham chunks (8 oz.)
1/2 C. Cheddar cheese,
  shredded

Combine eggs and milk in a bowl. Add onions, green pepper, mushrooms, ham, and cheese. Mix well and pour into unbaked pie crust.
Bake at 350 degrees for 40 to 50 minutes or until eggs are set. Set sit for 5 minutes. Serve with salsa if desired.

## SAUSAGE STACK
(oven or covered grill)

**English muffins**
**Cooked sausage patties**

**Pineapple slices**
**Cheddar cheese, shredded**

Toast English muffins. Top each half with a cooked sausage patty, a pineapple slice, and shredded cheese. Bake or grill until cheese is melted.

Recipe is also good with Canadian bacon or ham slice.

# SKILLET

## BREAKFAST MESS
(skillet)

**1/2 lb. bulk sausage**
**2 medium potatoes, sliced**
**6 eggs, beaten**

**1/2 small onion, chopped**
**1/2 small green pepper, chopped**
**Salsa (optional)**

Fry sausage in skillet until brown and crumbly. Remove sausage from skillet and set aside. Drain all but 2 T. sausage drippings from skillet. Fry potatoes, onions, and green pepper in 2 T. drippings until vegetables are tender. Add cooked sausage to skillet. Pour beaten eggs over all and cook, stirring, until eggs are done. Serve with salsa if desired.

This recipe can be made using ground beef or cubed ham instead of sausage, and hash browns can be used instead of potatoes. Great recipe for leftovers!

## MACARONI EGG SCRAMBLE
(skillet)

**1/2 small onion, chopped**
**1 T. vegetable oil**
**4 eggs**

**1/4 C. milk**
**1 C. cooked macaroni**
**1 C. canned luncheon meat, cubed**

In skillet, lightly brown chopped onion in oil. Beat eggs and milk in a bowl until well mixed. Add macaroni and luncheon meat to egg mixture. Put egg mixture in skillet. Cook over medium heat about 5 minutes or until eggs are cooked. Turn several times, but do not stir.

# BREAKFAST BOWLS FOR TWO (skillet)

2 eggs
2 C. frozen shredded hash
   browns
1/4 lb. bulk sausage
1 C. sausage gravy

1/4 small onion, chopped
1/4 green pepper, chopped
1/2 C. Cheddar cheese,
   shredded

Brown sausage in skillet; drain and set aside. In skillet, brown hash browns with onions and green peppers; remove from skillet and set aside. Beat each egg individually in a bowl and fry individually in skillet. Place an egg in each of two bowls. Divide the remaining ingredients in half and layer in the two bowls: hash browns mixture, sausage, sausage gravy, and cheese. Place in microwave and cook on high about 1 to 2 minutes, until heated throughout and cheese is melted.

This recipe can be put on plates instead of using bowls.


# PIEROGIES BREAKFAST (skillet)

8 oz. frozen potato pierogies
   (about 6 pierogies)
1/2 lb. bacon
4 eggs, beaten

1/2 C. Cheddar cheese, shredded
1/2 C. onion, chopped
1/2 C. green pepper, chopped

Fry bacon in skillet until browned. Drain on paper towels, reserving 1 T. of the fat. Break bacon into 1/2" pieces and set aside. Thaw pierogies in boiling water for 5 minutes; drain. In a bowl, combine eggs and 1/8 C. water; set aside. In skillet, sauté onion and green pepper in bacon drippings until tender. Add about 3/4 of the egg mixture to skillet; arrange pierogies over eggs; sprinkle bacon on top; and pour remaining egg mixture over all. Cover and cook over medium-low heat until eggs are set. Sprinkle with cheese and continue cooking until cheese is melted. Cut into wedges and serve.

This is a family favorite!

# OLD-FASHIONED ROAST BEEF HASH (skillet)

1/2 C. onion, chopped
2 T. butter
1/2 lb. deli roast beef, chopped
1/2 C. water

1 T. instant beef bouillon
1 tsp. Worcestershire sauce
1 T. flour
2 large potatoes

Peel and dice potatoes into 1/2" cubes. Cook in boiling water just until fork-tender (as if making potato salad). Drain potatoes and set aside. In a skillet, melt butter and cook onion until tender. Stir in roast beef, water, and bouillon. Cover and cook 10 minutes, stirring occasionally. Stir in flour and Worcestershire sauce. Add potatoes and stir gently. Cover and cook on medium heat for 5 minutes.

Excellent served with poached or fried eggs and toast! Leftover roast beef (about 2 C.) can be used in place of deli roast beef, if desired.

# SCRAMBLED EGGS AND MUSHROOMS (skillet)

1 lb. fresh mushrooms, sliced
1/2 C. butter
1/2 small onion, chopped

2 eggs, slightly beaten
2 T. sour cream

Heat butter in skillet. Add the mushrooms and onion; cook slowly, stirring occasionally, until onion is transparent and mushrooms are lightly browned and tender. Blend the eggs and sour cream thoroughly. Pour egg mixture into the skillet, mixing with the mushrooms and onions. Cook slowly over low heat, gently lifting the mixture from the sides of the skillet to allow the uncooked portion to flow to the bottom of the skillet. Avoid constant stirring. Cook until eggs are thick and creamy throughout, but still moist.

# FRIED ENGLISH MUFFINS (skillet)

English muffins
Pancake batter
Vegetable oil

Honey and butter (optional)
Powdered sugar and syrup
    (optional)
Maple syrup (optional)

Cut English muffin halves into quarters and dip in pancake batter. Fry in 1/4" of oil until lightly browned. Serve as desired with honey and butter, powdered sugar, or syrup.

# HARRY'S BREAKFAST TACOS

(skillet)

| | |
|---|---|
| 1 lb. bulk sausage or ground beef | 1-14 oz. can diced potatoes |
| 1-1 1/4 oz. env. taco seasoning | 1 doz. eggs |
| 1/2 small onion, chopped | Soft taco shells |
| 1/2 small green pepper, chopped | Salsa, sour cream (optional) |

Fry sausage (or ground beef), onion, and green pepper; drain. Add taco seasoning and diced potatoes. In another skillet, scramble eggs and add to sausage mixture. Serve on soft taco shells and top with salsa, cheese, and sour cream, if desired.

This recipe makes approximately 10 to 12 tacos. Leftovers can be frozen for later use.


# OPEN FACE OMELET

(skillet)

| | |
|---|---|
| 6 T. butter, divided | Dash of pepper |
| 3 C. frozen hash brown with onions and green peppers | 1/4 C. green onions, sliced |
| | 1/2 C. Cheddar cheese, shredded |
| 6 eggs | Bacon bits |
| 1/4 C. milk | Sour cream (optional) |
| 1/2 tsp. salt | |

Melt 3 T. butter in a skillet over medium heat. Add hash browns in an even layer. Cook potatoes, turning frequently about 10 minutes, or until tender and lightly browned. Set hash browns aside in a dish and keep warm. Meanwhile, in a bowl, beat eggs with milk, salt, and pepper. Melt remaining 3 T. butter in the same skillet. Pour in egg mixture and cook over medium heat, lifting edges as egg sets to allow uncooked portion to run underneath. When omelet is set, spoon the warm hash browns on top. Top with cheese, green onions, and bacon bits. Serve with sour cream, if desired.

# CINNAMON FRENCH TOAST (skillet)

3 eggs
1/4 C. milk
1/2 tsp. vanilla
1/2 tsp. ground cinnamon
1/8 tsp. ground nutmeg

6 slices Italian bread, cut diagonally
  1" thick
Cinnamon sugar (optional)
Maple syrup (optional)

In a bowl, beat eggs with a wire whisk. Add milk, vanilla, cinnamon, and nutmeg. Beat well; set aside. Lightly spray a nonstick skillet as needed with cooking spray; heat skillet over medium heat. Dip slices of bread into the egg mixture, coating both sides. Place bread slices in heated skillet. Cook until golden brown, turning once, about 1 to 2 minutes on each side. Serve with maple syrup and sprinkle with cinnamon sugar if desired.

Experiment with different types of bread in this recipe; cinnamon-raisin bread or whole-wheat bread works well. Try fruit preserves as a topping.


# OMELET TORTILLA ROLLUPS (skillet)

FOR TWO ROLLUPS:
2 flour tortillas
4 eggs
1/4 C. Cheddar cheese, shredded

1 C. shredded lettuce
4 T. thick salsa

Warm tortillas in skillet or between paper towels in microwave. Whisk 2 eggs in a bowl. Pour eggs into a nonstick 8" skillet over medium-high heat. Cook until set; gently turn over. Top with 1/8 C. cheese and cook until cheese is melted. Slide omelet onto warmed tortilla. Top with 1/2 C. lettuce and 2 T. salsa. Roll up into a cone shape or fold in half. Repeat above for second rollup.

Serve with a side of meat for breakfast, or with Spanish rice for dinner.

## ON-THE-RUN EGGS IN A PITA                          (skillet)

4 eggs                          2 pita pockets, toasted
2 T. milk                       4 T. Monterey jack cheese
2 tsp. butter                   2 T. thick salsa

Beat eggs and milk in a bowl.  Melt butter in a skillet; add egg mixture and cook, stirring, until done.  Cut opening at one side of pitas; fill with eggs.  Top with cheese and salsa.

This recipe makes 2 pita pockets.


## PANCAKES PLUS                          (skillet or griddle)

Pancake batter                  Your choice of additional
                                   ingredients

Add berries, sliced peaches, pineapple, chopped apples, nuts, raisins, or bits of ham, bacon, or sausage to prepared pancake batter; cook in skillet or on griddle.  Pancake batter can also be poured onto griddle and added ingredients above sprinkled on top.  Serve as desired with syrup or fruit preserves.

This recipe is a great way to use leftover breakfast meat.


# TOASTER


## FRENCH TOAST SANDWICH                          (toaster)

French toast slices, prepared        Cooked ham slices
   ahead of time and frozen
American cheese slices

Toast 2 frozen French toast slices in a toaster.  As soon as they pop up, place a slice of ham and a slice of cheese between them.  Wrap with a paper napkin to eat—napkin comes in handy for wiping fingers!

This is a great way to use leftover French toast.

# WAFFLE IRON

## WONDERFUL WAFFLES

(waffle iron)

1 3/4 C. flour
2 tsp. baking powder
1 T. sugar
1/2 tsp. salt
Maple syrup (optional)

3 egg yolks, beaten
1 1/2 C. milk
1/2 C. vegetable oil
3 egg whites, beaten stiff

Measure dry ingredients into mixing bowl; blend. Combine egg yolks and milk. Stir into dry ingredients. Stir in cooking oil. Carefully fold in egg whites. Do not over mix. Bake in a waffle iron according to manufacturer's instructions. Batter makes approximately 10 4x4" waffles.

TIP: Waffles can be frozen for later use. Freeze separately on a cookie sheet and store in a resealable storage bag. Reheat frozen waffles in a toaster.

---

## NOTES:

# NOTES:

_____

_____

_____

_____

_____

_____

_____

_____

_____

_____

_____

_____

_____

_____

_____

_____

_____

_____

# MAIN DISHES
# AND
# CASSEROLES

# My Favorites

## CHEESEBURGER POTATO PIE    Page 38

1 1/2 lb. lean ground beef
1/2 C. bread crumbs
1/4 C. onion, finely chopped
1/4 C. ketchup
2 tsp. mustard

1-32 oz. pkg. mashed potatoes
1 C. Cheddar cheese, shredded
1 medium tomato, chopped
2 green onions, sliced

Combine ground beef, bread crumbs, onion, ketchup, and mustard; mix well. Press mixture in bottom and up the sides of an ungreased 9" pie plate. Bake at 375 degrees for 15 minutes. Microwave mashed potatoes in a bowl on high for 2 to 3 minutes until warm *(Complete Recipe on page 38)*

## REUBEN CASSEROLE    Page 47

3 C. frozen hash browns
1/2 lb. deli corned beef,
sliced medium
1 T. vegetable oil

1-14 oz. can sauerkraut, drained
6 slices Swiss cheese
1/4 C. Russian salad dressing

Fully cook hash browns in oil in skillet, until hash browns are lightly browned and crispy. Spread cooked hash browns in bottom of a 9x9" pan. Cut corned beef into bite-size pieces and spread over hash *(Complete Receipe on page 47)*

# CROCK POT

## CROCK POT BEEF STROGANOFF

(crock pot)

2 lbs. beef stew meat
1-8 oz. can sliced mushrooms
1-10 3/4 oz. can cream of
  mushroomsoup
1-10 3/4 oz. can cream of celery
  soup

1-1 oz. env. dry onion soup mix
8 oz. sour cream
Cooked noodles

Spray crock pot with nonstick cooking spray. Combine stew meat, cream of mushroom soup, cream of celery soup, dry onion soup mix, and mushrooms (drained) in a 3 1/2-qt. crock pot. Cook on low 8 to 10 hours. One hour before serving, slowly add sour cream. Serve over cooked noodles.

TIP: 8 oz. of cream cheese can be substituted in place of sour cream.

## CROCK POT PIZZA

(crock pot)

1 1/2 lb. ground beef
1/2 medium onion, chopped
1 lb. uncooked rotini pasta (4 C.)
1-10 3/4 oz. can cream of
  mushroom soup
2-15 oz. cans pizza sauce
4 C. mozzarella cheese, shredded

1-8 oz. can sliced mushrooms,
  drained
1-3 oz. pkg. sliced pepperoni

Brown ground beef and onions; drain. Spray a 4-qt. crock pot with nonstick cooking spray. Making thin layers, layer following ingredients about halfway up crock pot: pizza sauce, ground beef, rotini, mushrooms, pepperoni, and cheese. Add 1/2 can of cream of mushroom soup, spreading evenly. Continue layering, saving about 1/2 C. cheese for topping. Over last layer, spread remaining 1/2 can soup and top with remaining 1/2 C. cheese. Cook about 8 hours on low, or until rotini is tender.

# CROCK POT SHIPWRECK

(crock pot)

2 large potatoes, peeled and
   sliced
1 1/2 lb. ground beef
2-10 3/4 oz. cans tomato soup

1 medium onion, sliced
1-15.5 oz. can kidney beans

Spray a 4-qt. crock pot with nonstick cooking spray. Spread one-half of the potatoes in bottom of crock pot, crumble one-half of the raw ground beef over potatoes. Top with one-half of the sliced onion. Drain kidney beans and sprinkle one-half of the can of beans over the onion. Gently spread one can of tomato soup over the top. Repeat layers. Cook 8 to 10 hours on low.


# BEEF POT PIE

(crock pot and oven)

2 lbs. beef round steak, cut
   in 1" cubes
3 T. flour
1 tsp. salt
1/8 tsp. black pepper
1-16 oz. can whole tomatoes,
   undrained

2 large potatoes, peeled
   and cubed
1 C. carrots, sliced
1 medium onion, chopped
1-32 oz. pkg. mashed potatoes

Spray crock pot with nonstick cooking spray. Place steak cubes in crock pot. Combine flour, salt, and pepper. Toss with steak to coat thoroughly. Stir in remaining ingredients except mashed potatoes. Cover and cook 8 to 10 hours on low. One hour before serving, remove meat and vegetables from crock pot and pour into a 3-qt. casserole dish. Top with mashed potatoes. Bake at 350 for 20 to 25 minutes or until potatoes are heated.

TIP: When using packaged mashed potatoes in a recipe, microwave potatoes in a bowl for about 2 minutes to soften, making them easier to handle. In this recipe, refrigerated biscuits can be used in place of the potatoes. Top with biscuits, and bake at 375 degrees for about 20 minutes or until biscuits are golden brown.

## DUTCH STUFFED PEPPERS

(oven or crock pot)

| | |
|---|---|
| 1 1/2 lb. ground beef | 3 T. rice, uncooked |
| 6 green peppers | 2 eggs, beaten |
| 1-10 3/4 oz. can tomato soup | 1/2 tsp. salt |

Mix meat, rice, eggs, and salt together. Cut tops off of peppers and discard. Soak peppers in hot water for a couple of minutes; scoop out seeds and fill with meat mixture. Stand peppers in a pan or put in a crock pot and cover with soup. Bake at 300 degrees for 1 hour or on low in crock pot for 6 to 8 hours.

# GRILL

## CAMPERS EASY PIZZA

(covered grill)

| | |
|---|---|
| Small  prebaked pizza crusts | Pizza sauce |
| Shredded mozzarella cheese | Toppings as desired |

Place pizza crusts on the grill and heat until warm, turning often to avoid burning. Remove from grill and cover with pizza sauce, toppings, and mozzarella cheese. Place on grill, cover, and cook until warm throughout and cheese is melted.

Have bowls of several toppings handy, and have fun letting each person make their own personal pizza. Suggested toppings: pepperoni, ground beef, ham, bacon, chopped onion, chopped green pepper, mushrooms, olives, sliced tomatoes.

# MICROWAVE

## SCALLOPED BOLOGNA BAKE

(microwave)

1-5 1/2 pkg. scalloped potato mix    1 lb. ring bologna

Skin ring bologna and cut into 3/4" slices. Use 1/4 C. less water than amount recommended on potato mix pkg. Put potatoes in a 2-qt. casserole dish; pour water over potatoes. Let stand 20 minutes. Add bologna slices, sauce mix, and milk (omit the butter). Cover. Microwave 10 to 15 minutes on 50% power or until potatoes are tender.

# TUNA POTATO BAKE

(microwave)

**4 medium potatoes**　　　　**2-6 oz. cans chunk tuna**
**2 T. mayonnaise**　　　　　**4 Cheddar cheese slices**

Scrub potatoes, puncture several times with a fork, and microwave on high until soft. Cut potatoes in half lengthwise and remove inside, leaving a shell. Mix removed potato with tuna and mayonnaise. Put back into potato shell, put in a pan or on a microwave-safe plate, and cover with slices of cheese. Microwave on high until cheese is melted.

Great for a main dish or for an easy brunch!

# OVEN

## SAVE A STEP LASAGNA

(oven)

**8 lasagna noodles, uncooked**　　**1 egg**
**1 C. cottage cheese**　　　　　　**1 lb. ground beef**
**1/2 medium onion, chopped**　　　**1/2 tsp. minced garlic**
**1-15 oz. can pizza sauce**　　　　**1-4 oz. can sliced mushrooms**
**1-l5 oz. can tomato sauce**　　　　**2 C. mozzarella cheese, shredded**
**1/2 C. Parmesan cheese**　　　　　**1 tsp. dried basil**

Cook ground beef in skillet until lightly browned. Add onion and cook until onion is tender; drain. Stir in pizza sauce, tomato sauce, drained mushrooms, basil, and garlic. Bring to a boil; reduce heat and simmer for 5 minutes. In a small bowl, combine cottage cheese and egg. Spray a 9x9" pan with nonstick cooking spray. Spread enough sauce in pan to cover the bottom (approximately 1/2 C.). Put 4 of the uncooked lasagna noodles in the pan, gently breaking as needed. Top with all of the cottage cheese, and layer with 1/2 C. mozzarella cheese, 1/4 C. Parmesan cheese, 1/2 of the sauce, then the remaining 4 lasagna noodles. Top with remaining sauce, mozzarella cheese, and Parmesan cheese. Cover tightly with foil and bake at 350 degrees for 45 minutes. Remove foil and continue baking for 15 minutes or until lightly browned. Let stand 15 minutes before cutting.

Bake this recipe without the hassle of cooking the noodles first!

## COUNTRY CHICKEN CASSEROLE

(oven)

1 C. milk
  Dressing (not mayonnaise)
2 C. cooked chicken chunks
5 oz. spaghetti

1-10 oz. pkg. frozen mixed
  vegetables
1/2 C. Miracle Whip Salad
1 lb. Velvetta cheese, cut into cubes

Cook spaghetti and mixed vegetables as directed on pkgs. and set aside. Combine milk and salad dressing until smooth. Add cubed Velvetta cheese. Stir over low heat until cheese is melted and sauce is smooth. Add drained spaghetti, drained vegetables, and chicken to cheese mixture. Mixture will be fairly runny. Pour into a 3-qt. casserole dish and bake at 350 degrees for 35 to 40 minutes.

It is very important to use salad dressing in this recipe—not real mayonnaise. The 5 oz. of spaghetti does not seem like much, but too much spaghetti will make this casserole too dry. The casserole will thicken during baking. Enjoy!

## STUFFED MEATLOAF

(oven)

2 lb. ground beef
1/2 green pepper, chopped
1/2 onion, chopped
1 C. bread crumbs, divided
1-6 oz. can tomato paste

1-4 oz. can sliced mushrooms
1 C. cottage cheese
1 T. dried parsley
3/4 C. mozzarella cheese, shredded
2 eggs

Combine ground beef, green pepper, onion, 3/4 C. bread crumbs, tomato paste, and eggs. Set aside. Combine cottage cheese, remaining 1/4 C. bread crumbs, mushrooms (drained) and parsley. Press one-half of the meat mixture in 9x9" pan. Cover with cottage cheese mixture. Then cover with remaining meat mixture. Bake at 350 degrees for 1 to 1 1/2 hours, until beef is no longer pink. Cover with mozzarella cheese and let sit for 6 to 10 minutes before serving.

This is a wonderful way to dress up an ordinary meatloaf!

# TURKEY CHEESE CASSEROLE(oven)

1-8 oz. jar cheese spread
1/2 C. milk
1 C. chopped cooked turkey
1-4 oz. can sliced mushrooms
1/4 tsp. onion salt

7 oz. spaghetti
1 10-oz. pkg. frozen chopped
  broccoli
2 T. green pepper, chopped
1/4 tsp. poultry seasoning
2 T. butter

Cook spaghetti and broccoli according to pkg. directions and set aside. Combine cheese and milk; mix well. Drain spaghetti and broccoli and toss spaghetti with butter. Combine all ingredients and put mixture into a 2 1/2-qt. casserole dish. Cover and bake at 350 degrees for 30 to 35 minutes. Stir before serving.

HINT: Spaghetti is easier to eat if broken into halves or thirds before cooking.

# CHEESEBURGER POTATO PIE(oven)

1 1/2 lb. lean ground beef
1/2 C. bread crumbs
1/4 C. onion, finely chopped
1/4 C. ketchup
2 tsp. mustard

1-32 oz. pkg. mashed potatoes
1 C. Cheddar cheese, shredded
1 medium tomato, chopped
2 green onions, sliced

Combine ground beef, bread crumbs, onion, ketchup, and mustard; mix well. Press mixture in bottom and up the sides of an ungreased 9" pie plate. Bake at 375 degrees for 15 minutes. Microwave mashed potatoes in a bowl on high for 2 to 3 minutes until warm and fluffy. Stir in 1/2 C. of the cheese. Remove beef crust from the oven and drain well, using paper towels to absorb the drippings. Spoon potato mixture evenly into crust. Return to oven and bake an additional 10 to 15 minutes or until beef is thoroughly cooked and potatoes are heated. Remove pie from oven. Top with remaining 1/2 C. cheese and tomato. Return to oven and bake an additional 5 minutes or until cheese is melted. Remove from oven and top with green onions. Let stand for 10 minutes. Cut into wedges and serve.

Instant potatoes may be used in place of the packaged mashed potatoes. Use 2 C. potato flakes, 1 1/4 C. water, and 3 T. butter; prepare according to pkg. directions.

# ENCHILADA CASSEROLE                    (oven)

12-6" tortilla shells
1 lb. ground beef
1/2 C. onions, chopped
1-8 oz. pkg. shredded lettuce

2 C. shredded Mexican cheese
2-10 oz. cans enchilada sauce
1/2 C. green pepper, chopped
Salsa and sour cream (optional)

Spray a 9x9" pan with nonstick cooking spray. Cook and drain the ground beef; set aside. Spread just enough enchilada sauce to lightly coat the bottom of the pan. Line with four tortilla shells (overlapping as needed). Cover with one-third of the shredded lettuce. Sprinkle with one-third of the onion and one-third of the green pepper. Top with one-third of the cooked meat, one-third of the cheese, and one-third of the enchilada sauce. Continue layers until all ingredients are used. Bake at 325 degrees for 45 minutes. Let stand 10 minutes before cutting. Serve with sour cream and salsa if desired.

Yes, you do bake the lettuce right in the casserole!

# MEATBALL SUB CASSEROLE                  (oven)

1/3 C. green onions, chopped
1/4 C. seasoned bread crumbs
3 T. grated Parmesan cheese
1 lb. ground beef
1/2 loaf Italian bread, cut into 1"
   slices
1-3 oz. pkg. cream cheese,
   softened

1/4 C. real mayonnaise
1/2 tsp. Italian seasoning
1/8 tsp. pepper
1 C. shredded mozzarella
   cheese, divided
1-14 oz. jar spaghetti sauce
1/2 C. water
1 tsp. minced garlic

In a bowl, combine green onions, bread crumbs, and Parmesan cheese. Add beef and mix well. Form into 1" balls; place in shallow pan. Bake at 350 degrees for 30 minutes or until no longer pink; drain. Meanwhile, arrange bread slices in a single layer in a 9x9" pan (all of bread may not be used). Combine cream cheese, mayonnaise, Italian seasoning, and pepper; spread over bread. Sprinkle with 1/2 C. mozzarella cheese. Place meatballs on top of mozzarella cheese. Combine spaghetti sauce, water, and garlic; pour over top of meatballs. Sprinkle with remaining mozzarella cheese. Bake uncovered at 350 degrees for 30 minutes.

TIP: Pre-cooked, frozen meatballs can be used in place of green onions, bread crumbs, Parmesan cheese, and ground beef. Thaw and cook frozen meatballs according to pkg. directions.

# SPAGHETTI CASSEROLE (oven)

1 lb. ground beef
3/4 C. onion, finely chopped
1/2 C. green pepper, chopped
8 oz. spaghetti
1-10 3/4 oz. can cream of
mushroom soup

1 soup can water
1-8 oz. can tomato sauce
1/2 tsp. minced garlic
1-10 3/4 oz. can tomato soup
1 C. Cheddar cheese, shredded

Cook ground beef in skillet until lightly browned. Add onion and green pepper and cook until vegetables are tender; drain. Stir in soups, water, tomato sauce, and garlic; heat through. Meanwhile, cook spaghetti according to pkg. directions and drain. Blend 1/2 C. of cheese and the spaghetti into the soup mixture. Put mixture into a 3-qt. casserole dish. Top with remaining 1/2 C. of cheese. Bake at 350 degrees for 45 minutes or until bubbly hot in the center.

Family favorite good enough to serve company! Serve with a side of garlic bread and a tossed salad.


# TUNA CASSEROLE (oven)

2-6 oz. cans chunk tuna
1/2 C. celery, chopped
1/2 C. sour cream
1/2 C. mayonnaise
3 C. uncooked egg noodles
1/4 tsp. salt

1/2 C. green onions, sliced
2 tsp. mustard
1 medium tomato, chopped
1 C. Monterey Jack cheese,
shredded

Drain and flake tuna, set aside. Cook noodles according to pkg. directions. Drain and rinse in hot water. Combine noodles with tuna, celery, and green onions. Blend in sour cream, mustard, mayonnaise, and salt. Spoon one-half of mixture into a 2-qt. casserole dish, sprayed with nonstick cooking spray. Top with cheese. Bake at 350 degrees for 30 minutes or until hot and bubbly. Sprinkle with tomato.

Wonderful served with a tossed salad and garlic bread!

# PRIZE WINNING BURRITO BAKE (oven)

1 C. all-purpose baking mix
1/4 C. water
1-16 oz. can refried beans
1 lb. ground beef

1 avocado, sliced (optional)
1 C. thick salsa
1 1/2 C. Cheddar cheese, shredded

Spray a 10" pie plate with nonstick cooking spray. Fry ground beef and drain well. Combine baking mix, water, and refried beans; spread in bottom of pie plate. Top with ground beef and layer avocado, salsa, and cheese on top of ground beef. Bake at 375 degrees for 30 minutes. Cut into wedges and serve with chopped tomatoes, guacamole, and sour cream if desired.

Top the meal off with a side of nacho chips and salsa!

# MACARONI AND BEEF BAKE (oven)

2 C. uncooked elbow macaroni
1/2 small onion, chopped
1-4 oz. can sliced mushrooms,
   drained
6 slices American cheese

1 lb. ground beef
2-10 3/4 oz. cans cream of
   mushroom soup
1/2 C. milk

Cook macaroni according to pkg. directions; drain. Meanwhile, cook ground beef until no longer pink, adding onions and mushrooms about halfway through cooking time; drain. Mix macaroni, ground beef mixture, soup and milk together. Put one-half of mixture in a 3-qt. casserole dish, sprayed with nonstick cooking spray. Top with 3 slices of cheese. Put remaining macaroni mixture in casserole dish, and top all with remaining 3 slices of cheese. Bake at 350 degrees for 20 to 30 minutes or until hot and cheese is melted.

# MEXICAN BEEF AND BEAN CASSEROLE     (oven)

1 lb. ground beef
2-15 oz. cans pinto beans
1-8 oz. can tomato sauce
1/2 C. chunky salsa

1 tsp. chili powder
1 C. Monterey Jack cheese,
  shredded

Brown ground beef; drain. Drain pinto beans and rinse. Mix beef, beans, tomato sauce, salsa, and chili powder in a 9x9" pan. Cover and bake at 375 degrees for 40 to 45 minutes, stirring once or twice, until hot and bubbly. Sprinkle cheese on top and bake, uncovered, for an additional 5 minutes, or until cheese is melted.


# TEXAS HASH     (oven)

1 lb. ground beef
1 large onion, sliced
1 large green pepper, chopped
1-16 oz. can tomatoes

1/2 C. uncooked regular rice
2 tsp. salt
2 tsp. chili powder
1/8 tsp. pepper

In large skillet, cook and stir ground beef, onion, and green pepper until meat is browned and vegetables are tender; drain. Stir in tomatoes, rice, salt, chili powder, and pepper; heat throughout. Pour into a 2-qt casserole dish. Cover and bake at 350 degrees for 1 hour.


# PORK CHOP AND POTATO CASSEROLE     (oven)

4 pork chops
4 C. frozen hash browns
  (do not thaw)
1/2 C. sour cream
1-10 3/4 oz. can cream of
  celery soup

1/4 tsp. pepper
1/2 tsp. seasoned salt
1 C. Cheddar cheese, shredded,
  divided
1-3 oz. can French fried onion
  rings, divided

In a bowl, mix frozen hash browns, sour cream, soup, salt, pepper, 1/2 C. cheese, and 1/2 can onion rings. Put mixture in bottom of a 9x9" pan sprayed with nonstick cooking spray. Brown pork chops and place on top of potato mixture. Cover with foil and bake at 350 degrees for 45 to 60 minutes. Uncover and sprinkle with remaining 1/2 can of onion rings and remaining 1/2 C. cheese. Bake an additional 5 minutes or until cheese is melted.

TIP: Heat leftover potatoes and serve as a side dish with breakfast!

## VEGETABLE BEEF CASSEROLE (oven)

1/2 C. onion, chopped
1 1/2 lb. ground beef
1-28 oz. can whole tomatoes
1-6 oz. can tomato paste

1-16 oz. pkg. frozen mixed
   vegetables
1 C. water
1-12 oz. pkg. refrigerated biscuits

Brown ground beef and onions in a skillet; drain. Add tomatoes, tomato paste, water, and frozen vegetables. Bring to a boil; simmer 15 minutes. Remove from heat. Spoon into a 3-qt casserole dish. Arrange biscuits on top. Bake at 375 degrees for 15 to 20 minutes, or until biscuits are lightly browned. Let stand 10 minutes before serving.

Mashed potatoes can be used in place of biscuits in this recipe. Put mashed potatoes on top and sprinkle with about 1 C. Cheddar cheese. Bake until potatoes are lightly browned and cheese is melted. Let stand 10 minutes before serving.

## CUBE STEAK AND MUSHROOM CASSEROLE
(oven)

4 cube steaks
2/3 C. milk
2 T. bacon drippings
2 medium onions, sliced
8 oz. fresh mushrooms, sliced
1-10 3/4 oz. can golden
   mushroom soup

1 T. minced parsley
1 tsp. salt
1/4 tsp. pepper
1/4 tsp. dry mustard
4 medium potatoes, sliced

In skillet, brown steaks in bacon drippings. Remove steaks from skillet and set aside. Sauté onions and mushrooms in skillet until tender; drain. Combine soup, milk, parsley, salt, pepper, and dry mustard. Place alternate layers of potatoes, onions, mushrooms, and steaks in a 2 1/2-qt. greased casserole dish or square pan, pouring a small amount of soup over each layer. Cover with foil and bake at 350 degrees for 1 to 1 1/2 hours, or until potatoes are tender.

## HAMBURGER DRESSING BAKE    (oven)

1 lb. ground beef
6 slices of toast, cubed
3 eggs, beaten

1/4 sm. onion, chopped
1 stalk celery, chopped
Salt & pepper to taste

Brown ground beef, onions, and celery in a skillet; drain. Combine beef mixture, toast cubes, eggs, salt and pepper. Put in a casserole dish and bake at 350 degrees for 30 minutes.

For a quick and easy dinner, serve with a side of vegetables and a tossed salad


## STUFFED PIZZA    (oven)

2-12" frozen cheese pizzas,
  thin crust
1/4 C. each chopped green,
  peppers onions, mushrooms
Olive oil

1 lb. ground beef
1 C. mozzarella cheese,
  shredded

Fry ground beef and vegetables; drain. Put a large piece of aluminum foil on a pizza pan, large enough to wrap the pizza. Place one pizza on the foil. Top with ground beef and vegetables. Place second pizza UPSIDE DOWN on top of first pizza. Wrap in foil, seal well. Bake at 375 degrees for 20 to 25 minutes. Open foil, brush top of pizza with olive oil, and cover with mozzarella cheese. Bake uncovered an additional 15 minutes or until cheese is melted.


## IMPOSSIBLE HAM 'N SWISS PIE    (oven)

2 C. cooked ham, chopped
1 C. Swiss cheese, shredded
1/3 C. onion, chopped

4 eggs
2 C. milk
1 C. all-purpose baking mix

Spray 10" pie plate with nonstick cooking spray. Sprinkle ham, cheese, and onions in pie plate. Beat eggs, milk, and baking mix with hand mixer or blender until smooth; continue beating for 1 minute. Pour into pie plate. Bake at 375 degrees for 40 to 45 minutes until lightly browned and a knife inserted in the center comes out clean. Cool 5 minutes.

# SPAGHETTI PIE

(oven)

6 oz. spaghetti
2 T. butter
2 eggs, well-beaten
1/3 C. Parmesan cheese
1 lb. ground beef
1-14 oz. can spaghetti sauce

1/2 C. onion, chopped
1/4 C. green pepper, chopped
1 C. cottage cheese
1 1/2 C. mozzarella cheese,
   shredded

Cook spaghetti as directed on pkg.; drain and rinse with hot water. Stir in butter, Parmesan cheese, and eggs. Press into a 10" pie plate, sprayed with nonstick cooking spray. Brown ground beef, onion, and green peppers; drain. Add spaghetti sauce to ground beef mixture; mix well. Simmer 10 minutes. Spread cottage cheese on top of spaghetti. Top with meat sauce. Bake at 350 degrees for 20 minutes. Top with mozzarella cheese and bake an additional 5 minutes, or until cheese is melted.


# TACO PIE

(oven)

1-4 oz. pkg. crescent rolls (4 rolls)
1 lb. ground beef
1-1 1/4 oz. pkg. taco seasoning
8 oz. sour cream
1-16 oz. can refried beans
1 C. salsa

1 C. crushed tortilla chips
1 C. Cheddar cheese,
   shredded
Shredded lettuce
Chopped tomatoes

Press crescent rolls into a 9x9" pan, sprayed with nonstick cooking spray, to form a crust. Brown ground beef; drain well. Add taco seasoning, sour cream, refried beans, and salsa to ground beef; mix well. Spread mixture over crescent rolls. Sprinkle top with crushed tortilla chips. Bake at 350 degrees for 25 minutes. Top with cheese and bake an additional 5 to 10 minutes or until cheese is melted. Serve with shredded lettuce and chopped tomatoes.

## LAYERED MEAT-VEGETABLE CASSEROLE                (oven)

1 lb. ground beef
1-8 oz. can tomato sauce
1 green pepper, chopped
1 C. cooked rice
1/4 C. sliced green olives
5 oz. frozen peas, thawed

2 hard-boiled eggs, cut in wedges
4 servings instant mashed potatoes,
   prepared according to pkg.
   directions
1/2 C. Cheddar cheese, shredded

Brown ground beef; drain.  Add tomato sauce and green peppers.
Cover and simmer for 15 minutes.  Add cooked rice; mix well.  Put
one-half of the meat mixture in a 2 1/2-qt. casserole dish, sprayed
with nonstick cooking spray.  Layer olives and eggs on top.  Layer
remaining meat mixture, then peas.  Combine mashed potatoes with
cheese; spread on top of peas.  Bake at 375 for 30 minutes or until top
is browned.


## DEEP DISH TACO SQUARES                          (oven)

1/2 lb. ground beef
1/2 C. sour cream
1/3 C. mayonnaise
1/2 C. Cheddar cheese,
   shredded
1/2 C. green pepper, chopped

1 C. all-purpose baking mix
1/4 C. cold water
1 to 2 medium tomatoes, thinly slice
1 T. onion, chopped

Cook ground beef until brown; drain.  Mix sour cream, mayonnaise,
cheese, and onions; set aside.  Combine baking mix and water until
soft dough forms.  Pat dough in an 8x8" pan, sprayed with nonstick
cooking spray, pressing dough 1/2" up sides of pan.  Layer beef,
tomatoes, and green pepper in pan.  Spoon sour cream mixture over
top.  Sprinkle with paprika if desired.  Bake at 375 degrees for 25 to 30
minutes, or until edges of dough are light browned.

# KING RANCH CHICKEN
(oven)

3 large chicken breasts, cooked
 and chopped
1 C. cooked rice
1/4 C. picante sauce
1 C. onion, chopped
1 T. butter

1 C. celery, chopped
1-10 3/4 oz. can cream of mushroom
 soup
2 C. Cheddar cheese, shredded
1 C. chow mein noodles

Sauté onions and celery in butter and picante sauce until tender. Add chicken and soup. Put cooked rice in a 2 1/2-qt. casserole dish, sprayed with nonstick cooking spray. Cover with chicken mixture. Top with cheese. Bake at 350 degrees for 30 minutes. Sprinkle with chow mein noodles and bake an additional 5 minutes

# KRAUT AND SAUSAGE CASSEROLE
(oven)

1 lb. bulk sausage
Mashed potatoes (made in
 advance from 4 med. potatoes)
 shredded

1-14 oz. can sauerkraut
1 1/2 C. mozzarella cheese,

Brown sausage; drain. Place sausage in bottom of a 9x9" pan, sprayed with nonstick cooking spray. Spoon mashed potatoes on top of sausage and carefully spread evenly. Drain sauerkraut and spread on top of potatoes. Bake at 350 degrees for 20 minutes. Top casserole with mozzarella cheese and bake an additional 10 minutes or until cheese is melted.

# REUBEN CASSEROLE
(oven)

3 C. frozen hash browns
1/2 lb. deli corned beef,
 sliced medium
1 T. vegetable oil

1-14 oz. can sauerkraut, drained
6 slices Swiss cheese
1/4 C. Russian salad dressing

Fully cook hash browns in oil in skillet, until hash browns are lightly browned and crispy. Spread cooked hash browns in bottom of a 9x9" pan. Cut corned beef into bite-size pieces and spread over hash browns. Spread Russian salad dressing over meat. Spoon drained sauerkraut over top. Cover with slices of cheese, overlapping or cutting as necessary. Bake at 350 degrees for 30 minutes. Serve with Russian dressing on the side if desired.

# EASY SHEPHERD'S PIE

(oven)

1 lb. ground beef
1/2 C. onion, chopped
1-15 oz. can mixed vegetables,
  drained
1-15 oz. can stewed tomatoes,
  drained
1 C. Cheddar cheese, shredded

1-15 oz. can Italian-style
  tomato sauce
6 servings instant mashed
  potatoes, prepared
  according to pkg.
  directions

Brown ground beef and onions; drain. Add mixed vegetables, stewed tomatoes, and tomato sauce to beef. Put in a 2-qt. casserole dish, sprayed with nonstick cooking spray. Spoon prepared mashed potatoes on top of beef mixture. Carefully spread potatoes evenly with the back of a spoon. Bake at 350 degrees for 25 minutes. Sprinkle cheese on top of potatoes and bake an additional 5 minutes or until cheese is melted.


# TATER TOT HOT DISH

(oven or microwave)

1 1/2 lb. lean ground beef
1-16 oz. pkg. frozen tater tot
  potatoes
2-15 oz. cans mixed vegetables,
  drained

2-10 3/4 oz. cans cream of
  mushroom soup

Fry ground beef until no longer pink; drain. Mix beef, soup, and drained mixed vegetables together and place in a 2 1/2-qt. casserole dish. Place tater tots on top. Bake at 350 degrees for 45 minutes.

To microwave, lightly spread raw ground beef in bottom of a 9x9" pan. Spread soup on top of beef. Sprinkle mixed vegetables on top of soup. Top with tater tots. Microwave on high for 10 to 11 minutes or until soup is bubbly and beef is firm. Let stand 3 to 5 minutes.

# SKILLET

## SOUTHERN CHILI MAC (skillet)

1-7 1/4 oz. box macaroni and
  cheese dinner
1-8 oz. can tomato sauce

1-15 oz. can whole kernel
  corn, drained
1-15 oz. can chili with beans

In a skillet, make macaroni and cheese dinner according to pkg. directions. Add drained corn, chili, and tomato sauce. Mix well. Heat for about 5 minutes or until warm throughout.

Great served with hot dogs or with a salad and garlic toast!

## MEXICAN CHICKEN AND BEANS (skillet)

1 T. vegetable oil
1 1/4 lb. boneless skinless
  chicken breasts
2 tsp. chili powder
1-15 oz. can pinto beans

1-11 oz. can whole kernel corn
Salsa (optional)
Flour tortillas (optional)
Sour cream (optional)

Cut chicken into 1" pieces. Heat oil in skillet and cook chicken pieces over medium heat until no longer pink, stirring occasionally. Drain pinto beans and rinse. Add drained beans, chili powder, and undrained corn to chicken. Cook over medium heat 4 to 5 minutes, stirring frequently until hot. Serve with salsa, tortillas, and sour cream, if desired.

## SLOPPY JOE ROTINI (skillet)

1 lb. ground beef
2 C. uncooked rotini pasta
1-15 1/2 oz. jar thick sloppy joe
  sauce

2 C. frozen whole kernel corn
1 C. water

Cook beef in skillet, drain well. Stir in remaining ingredients. Heat to boiling. Reduce heat, cover, and simmer approximately 15 minutes or until pasta is tender, stirring occasionally.

# STOVETOP

## CHILI CHEESE PIEROGIES     (stovetop)

**1-16 oz. pkg. frozen potato pierogies**
**8 oz. Cheddar cheese, shredded**

**2-15 oz. cans of chili**
**16 oz. sour cream**

Thaw pierogies in boiling water for 5 minutes; drain and set aside. Meanwhile, heat chili in a saucepan. Place pierogies on a serving platter, top with chili, sprinkle with cheese, and top with sour cream.

## MACARONI GOULASH WITH PEPPERONI     (stovetop)

**1 1/2 lb. ground beef**
**3 C. uncooked elbow macaroni**
**1-28 oz. can pizza sauce**
**1/2 small onion, chopped**

**1-26 oz. can spaghetti sauce**
**1 C. sliced pepperoni**
**1-8 oz. can mushrooms, drained**

Brown ground beef and onions; drain. Cook macaroni according to pkg. directions; drain. Combine all ingredients and cook over medium heat until warm throughout. Serve with garlic bread.

## NOTES:

_____

_____

_____

_____

_____

_____

_____

_____

# MEAT, POULTRY
# AND
# SEAFOOD

# My Favorites

## PORCUPINE MEATBALLS

Page 61

1 1/2 lb. ground beef
1/2 C. uncooked instant rice
1/4 tsp. pepper
1/2 tsp. seasoned salt
1/4 tsp. garlic powder

1/4 C. onion, finely chopped
2 tsp. vegetable oil
1 C. water
1-15 oz. can tomato sauce

Mix together ground beef, rice, onion, pepper, seasoned salt, and garlic powder. Form into 1 1/2" balls. Brown meatballs in oil in a hot skillet. Add tomato sauce and water.
*(Complete Recipe on page 61)*

## CHICKEN GOURMET DINNER

Page 56

4 boneless, skinless chicken breasts
1/2 bunch broccoli
4 oz. Swiss cheese, sliced
1-10 3/4 oz. can cream of chicken soup
1-10 3/4 oz. can cream of celery soup

1-10 3/4 oz. can cream of mushroom soup
1-6 oz. box of chicken-flavored stuffing mix

Prepare stuffing according to pkg. directions. Blend soups together. Put 1/3 of the soup mixture in the bottom of a 9x9" pan, sprayed with nonstick cooking spray. Layer chicken, cheese slices, 1/3 soup *(Complete Recipe on page 56)*

# CROCK POT

## CROCK POT "FRIED" CHICKEN

(crock pot)

1 (2 to 3 lb.) whole chicken,
  cut in pieces
1 C. flour
1 tsp. salt
1 tsp. paprika

1 tsp. dried oregano
1/4 tsp. garlic powder
Dash pepper
1 stick butter

Rinse chicken and pat dry with paper towels. In a plastic sealable storage bag, combine flour with remaining ingredients except butter. In a skillet, melt butter. Place 2 or 3 pieces of chicken into flour mixture, seal bag, and toss until coated. Remove chicken, shaking off excess flour. Repeat with remaining chicken. Cook chicken in butter over medium-high heat until golden brown (about 10 minutes on each side). Spray a 4-qt. crock pot with nonstick cooking spray. Place browned chicken in crock pot, skin side up. Do not add liquid. Cover and cook on low 8 to 10 hours.

This recipe really works! Do not add liquid to crock pot, and try to resist all temptation to "peek" during cooking time!

## EASY SWISS STEAK

(crock pot)

2 lbs. beef round steak, about
  1" thick
1 small onion, sliced thin

1-15 oz. cans stewed tomatoes
1/2 tsp. garlic powder

Cut round steak into serving-size pieces. Place in a 3 1/2-qt. crock pot, sprayed with nonstick cooking spray. Spread sliced onions on top of meat. Sprinkle with garlic powder. Top with stewed tomatoes (undrained). Cover and cook on low 8 to 10 hours.

Serve with mashed potatoes or rice.

# CHICKEN BREASTS AND SWEET POTATOES

(crock-pot)

4 boneless, skinless chicken breasts
1-10 3/4 oz. cream of chicken soup
2/3 C. flour
1 tsp. seasoned salt
1/2 tsp. garlic powder
1/2 tsp. paprika
Dash pepper
2 medium sweet potatoes
3 T. flour
1-4 oz. can mushrooms, drained
1/2 C. orange juice
2 tsp. brown sugar
Hot buttered rice

Peel sweet potatoes and cut into 1/4" slices. Put sweet potatoes in bottom of a 4-qt. crock pot, sprayed with nonstick cooking spray. In a plastic sealable storage bag, combine 2/3 C. flour, seasoned salt, garlic powder, paprika, and pepper. Rinse chicken breasts and pat dry with paper towels. Place 2 pieces of chicken into flour mixture, seal bag, and toss until chicken is coated. Remove chicken, shaking off excess flour, and place on top of sweet potatoes. Repeat with remaining chicken. In a bowl, combine soup, mushrooms, orange juice, brown sugar, and 3 T. flour. Pour soup mixture over chicken. Cover and cook 8 to 10 hours on low. Serve with rice.


# BEEF AND NOODLES

(crock pot)

1/2 C. plus 3 T. flour, divided
1 tsp. salt
1/8 tsp. pepper
4 lbs. beef stew meat
2-4 oz. cans sliced mushrooms
1/2 C. green onions, sliced
1-10 1/2 oz. can beef broth
1 tsp. ketchup
1 tsp. Worcestershire sauce
1/4 C. water
Cooked noodles

Combine 1/2 C. flour, salt and pepper; toss with beef to coat thoroughly—a plastic storage bag works well for this. Place meat in a 3 1/2-qt. crock pot, sprayed with nonstick cooking spray. Drain mushrooms and add mushrooms and green onions to crock pot. In a bowl, combine beef broth, ketchup, and Worcestershire sauce. Pour over beef and vegetables; stir well. Cook on low 8 to 12 hours. One hour before serving, turn to high. Make a smooth paste of water and 3 T. flour; slowly stir into crock pot and mix well. Continue cooking until thickened. Serve over hot noodles.

## SPANISH CHICKEN 'N OLIVES

(crock pot)

| | |
|---|---|
| 3 lb. chicken pieces | 3/4 C. beer |
| Salt and pepper | 1/2 C. sliced green olives |
| 1-8 oz. can tomato sauce | 1/2 tsp. minced garlic |
| 1 large onion, chopped | Hot cooked rice |

Rinse chicken pieces and pat dry with paper towels. Lightly season with salt and pepper. In a bowl, combine tomato sauce, chopped onion, beer, green olives, and garlic. Put chicken in a 3 1/2-qt. or 4-qt. crock pot, sprayed with nonstick cooking spray. Add tomato sauce mixture and gently stir to coat all chicken pieces; or put chicken in the crock pot, several pieces at a time, and pour part of the tomato sauce mixture over each layer. Cook on low for 7 to 9 hours. Serve over cooked rice.

## TINA'S CHICKEN AND STUFFING

(crock pot)

| | |
|---|---|
| 4 boneless, skinless chicken breasts | 1-10 3/4 oz. can cream of chicken soup |
| 1-6 oz. box stuffing mix | |
| 3 C. Cheddar cheese, shredded | |

Prepare stuffing according to pkg. directions. Put in a 3 1/2-qt. crock pot sprayed with nonstick cooking spray. Put chicken on top of stuffing. Cover chicken with soup. Sprinkle cheese on top. Cook on low for 5 to 6 hours or until chicken is done.

# GRILL

## DIJON CHICKEN KABOBS

(grill)

| | |
|---|---|
| 1/2 C. Dijon mustard | 1/4 C. fresh parsley, minced |
| 1 tsp. green onion, chopped fine | 1 1/4 lb. chicken breasts, cut in pieces |
| 2 C. fresh bread crumbs | |

In a bowl, mix Dijon mustard and green onion. In another bowl, mix bread crumbs and parsley. Dip chicken pieces in mustard mixture; then dip in bread crumbs mixture. Put chicken on skewers and grill for about 10 minutes, or until chicken is done.

## CAMPFIRE MUSTARD ROAST

(grill or open fire)

1 chuck roast                    Mustard

Cover chuck roast generously with mustard on all sides. Put in a container and let marinate overnight. Cook over a grill or open fire to desired doneness, similar to cooking a steak. Do not remove mustard before cooking.

This recipe works well with an inexpensive cut of beef; mustard works as a tenderizer.

# OVEN

## FISH STICK TACOS

(oven)

12 frozen fish sticks            Shredded lettuce
6 soft taco shells               Tomato, chopped
1/3 C. mayonnaise                Salsa (optional)
1 T. taco seasoning

Cook fish sticks as directed on pkg. Combine mayonnaise and taco seasoning; mix well. Carefully cut each warm fish stick into 3 or 4 pieces. Spread one side of each heated taco shell with mayonnaise mixture. Top half of each with fish sticks, lettuce, and tomato. Fold over and serve with salsa if desired.

## CHICKEN GOURMET DINNER

(oven)

4 boneless, skinless chicken        1-10 3/4 oz. can cream of
  breasts                         mushroom soup
1/2 bunch broccoli                  1-6 oz. box of chicken-
4 oz. Swiss cheese, sliced            flavored stuffing mix
1-10 3/4 oz. can cream of chicken
  soup
1-10 3/4 oz. can cream of celery
  soup

Prepare stuffing according to pkg. directions. Blend soups together. Put 1/3 of the soup mixture in the bottom of a 9x9" pan, sprayed with nonstick cooking spray. Layer chicken, cheese slices, 1/3 soup mixture, and broccoli. Top with remaining 1/3 soup mixture and cover with dressing. Bake at 350 degrees for 1 hour.

# POTATO CHIP CHICKEN FINGERS

(oven)

**3 boneless, skinless chicken
breasts
1-6 oz. pkg. potato chips**

**2 eggs
4 T. milk**

Cut chicken breasts into finger-size pieces. Fill a large plastic sealable bag with potato chips; seal the bag, and crush the chips. In a bowl, whisk the egg and milk. Dip the chicken pieces into the egg mixture, then into the bag of chips. Shake gently to cover. Place in a shallow baking pan. Bake at 375 degrees for 20 to 25 minutes, flipping over once during cooking time. Serve with a dipping sauce such as Ranch salad dressing or barbecue sauce.

Any flavor of potato chips can be used—try plain, barbecue, or sour cream chips.


# CINCINNATI CHICKEN

(oven)

**1-16 oz. can whole cranberry
sauce
1-8 oz. bottle Russian salad
dressing
4 boneless, skinless chicken breasts**

**1-1 oz. env. dry onion soup
mix
Cooked rice or noodles**

Combine cranberry sauce, salad dressing, and soup mix. Arrange chicken in a 3-qt. casserole dish. Pour sauce over chicken. Cover and bake at 325 degrees for 1 hour. Remove cover and continue baking for 15 minutes. Serve over rice or noodles.


# MEXICAN CHICKEN

(oven)

**4 boneless, skinless chicken
breasts
4 oz. Cheddar cheese, shredded**

**1-5 oz. pkg. tortilla chips
1-8 oz. jar salsa**

In a 9x9" pan, sprayed with nonstick cooking spray, layer the tortilla chips and top with chicken. Cover with salsa and sprinkle with cheese. Bake at 350 degrees for 30 to 40 minutes. Serve with sour cream, if desired.

# SIMPLE SALISBURY STEAKS  (oven)

1 lb. ground beef
1/3 C. bread crumbs
1-10 3/4 oz. can cream of
  mushroom soup, divided

1 egg, beaten
1/4 C. onion, finely chopped
1-8 oz. can sliced mushrooms

Mix 1/4 C. mushroom soup, ground beef, bread crumbs, egg, and onion. Make patties and brown on both sides. Put patties in a casserole dish. Mix remaining soup and mushrooms; pour over meat. Cover and bake in 250 degree over for 1 1/2 to 2 hours.

Patties can be grilled first for a wonderful grilled flavor. If you want more gravy, use 2 cans of cream of mushroom soup. Great served with mashed potatoes!

# POOR MAN'S STEAK  (oven)

1 1/2 lb. ground beef
1/2 C. bread crumbs
1-10 3/4 can cream mushroom
  soup
Flour

1/2 C. milk
1/2 sm. onion, chopped
1/2 soup can water
1/2 soup can milk

Combine ground beef, 1/2 C. milk, bread crumbs, and onion. Spread mixture into bottom of a 9x9" pan or plastic container. Cover and refrigerate at least 3 hours or overnight. Cut meat into squares. Lightly flour beef squares and brown in a skillet; put in a 9x9" pan. Mix soup, 1/2 soup can water, and 1/2 soup can of milk. Cover beef with soup mixture. Bake at 375 degrees for 1 hour.

For different flavors, try using golden mushroom soup, or cream of celery soup.

# SKILLET

## TUNA CAKES

(skillet)

2-6 oz. cans tuna, drained and
 flaked
1/2 C. seasoned bread crumbs
1/4 tsp. ground red pepper
4 buns, split

3/4 C. mayonnaise, divided
2 T. green onions, chopped
2 T. green pepper, chopped

Reserve 1/4 C. mayonnaise to spread on buns. Combine remaining 1/2 C. mayonnaise, tuna, bread crumbs, green onion, ground red pepper, and green pepper; mix lightly. Shape into 4 patties. Cook patties in skillet on medium heat for 2 to 3 minutes or until golden brown on each side. Spread buns with reserved mayonnaise and fill with tuna cakes.

Tuna cakes can also be served without the buns as a main dish with a side of cole slaw.

## CHICKEN STUFFING SKILLET

(skillet)

1 T. butter
4 boneless, skinless chicken
 breasts
1-6 oz. box chicken flavored stuffing
 mix
1/2 C. milk

1/2 C. Cheddar cheese, shredded
1-10 3/4 oz. can cream of
 celery soup

Heat butter in skillet. Add chicken breasts and cook until done. Remove chicken and wipe out skillet. In same skillet, prepare stuffing mix according to pkg. directions except let stand only 2 minutes. In a small saucepan, mix soup and milk; heat until warm. Place chicken on top of stuffing; pour soup mixture over chicken. Sprinkle with cheese. Cover and let sit until cheese is melted.

TIP: When cooking with butter or margarine, add 1 tsp. oil to prevent butter or margarine from burning.

## ONE-PAN CHICKEN AND POTATOES (skillet)

1 lb. boneless, skinless chicken
  breasts
8 medium red potatoes, sliced thin
2 T. vegetable oil

1 medium red bell pepper
1 tsp. garlic salt

Cut chicken in thin strips. Slice red bell pepper in thin strips. Heat oil in a skillet. Add potatoes, chicken, and red bell pepper. Sprinkle with garlic salt. Cook for 15 to 20 minutes, stirring frequently or until chicken is done and potatoes are tender.


## BACON STUFFED CHICKEN BREASTS (skillet)

4 large boneless, skinless
  chicken breasts
4 slices bacon, cooked
4 T. Cheddar cheese, shredded

2 T. olive oil
1-14 oz. can diced tomatoes
  with Italian herbs
1 C. water

Lay chicken breast on a cutting board. With knife blade parallel to board, slice chicken almost all the way through. Open breast like a book. Repeat with remaining chicken. On each chicken breast, spread 1 T. shredded cheese near the fold, leaving a 1/2" border around the edge. For each chicken breast, break 1 slice cooked bacon into bite-size pieces and place on top of cheese. Fold chicken breasts over; place on plate. Cover with plastic wrap and freeze for 30 minutes. To cook, heat olive oil in skillet over medium high heat. Add chicken and cook about 5 minutes on each side until lightly browned. Add diced tomatoes and water to skillet. Reduce heat, cover, and simmer 30 minutes, stirring occasionally.


## HASH TACOS (skillet)

1-15 oz. can roast beef hash
1 C. tomatoes, chopped
1/2 C. green pepper, chopped
1 tsp. chili powder

Shredded lettuce
Cheddar cheese, shredded
Salsa
Taco shells

Heat hash in skillet. Add tomatoes, green peppers, and chili powder; mix thoroughly. Spoon into heated taco shells. Garnish as desired with lettuce, cheese, and salsa.

# RANCH CHICKEN                     (skillet)

**4 boneless, skinless chicken**
  **breasts**
**1/3 C. Ranch salad dressing**

**3/4 C. bread crumbs**
**2 T. olive or vegetable oil**

Rinse chicken under cold water and pat dry with paper towels. Dip chicken into salad dressing, coating all sides. Coat all sides with bread crumbs. Heat oil in skillet over medium-high heat. Cook chicken in oil 15 minutes, turning over once, until outside is golden brown and juice is no longer pink.

Chicken can also be baked in a 350 degree oven for 20 to 30 minutes, instead of frying.


# PORCUPINE MEATBALLS                 (skillet)

**1 1/2 lb. ground beef**
**1/2 C. uncooked instant rice**
**1/4 tsp. pepper**
**1/2 tsp. seasoned salt**
**1/4 tsp. garlic powder**

**1/4 C. onion, finely chopped**
**2 tsp. vegetable oil**
**1 C. water**
**1-15 oz. can tomato sauce**

Mix together ground beef, rice, onion, pepper, seasoned salt, and garlic powder. Form into 1 1/2" balls. Brown meatballs in oil in a hot skillet. Add tomato sauce and water. Cover skillet and simmer on low heat for 45 minutes or until rice is tender. Uncover and simmer an additional 5 to 10 minutes to thicken sauce. Serve meatballs as a main dish or with spaghetti. Serve on hoagie buns topped with mozzarella cheese for wonderful meatball subs!

## CHICKEN AND STUFFING DINNER                    (skillet)

4 boneless chicken breasts
1 T. butter
1-6 oz. box stuffing mix
   shredded
1-10 3/4 oz. can cream of celery
   soup

1/2 C. milk
1/2 C. Cheddar cheese,

Heat butter in skillet.  Cook chicken in butter 15 minutes or until done.
Remove chicken and set aside.  Prepare stuffing in skillet according
to pkg. directions, except let stand for 2 minutes.  Top stuffing with
chicken.  Mix soup and milk together and pour over chicken.  Sprinkle
with cheese.  Cover and cook until heated throughout and cheese is
melted.


# <u>STOVETOP</u>


## EASY CHICKEN ALA KING                          (stovetop)

2 boneless, skinless chicken
   breasts, cooked and cubed
2-18 oz. jars chicken gravy

1 lb. frozen mixed vegetables
Biscuits

Cook mixed vegetables according to pkg. directions; drain.  Combine
chicken, vegetables, and gravy in a saucepan; heat.  Serve over
biscuits.

_____

# NOTES:

_____

_____

_____

_____

_____

# FOIL COOKING

# My Favorites

## SHIPWRECK IN FOIL — Page 66

PER SERVING:
1/4 lb. ground beef
1 small potato, sliced
2 slices of onion

1/2-14 oz. can kidney beans
1/2-10 3/4 oz. can tomato soup
Salt, pepper, garlic powder to taste

Place sliced potato on a large piece of heavy-duty aluminum foil, sprayed with nonstick cooking spray. Crumble raw ground beef over potato. Layer onion slices and kidney beans (drained) on top of *(Complete Recipe on page 66)*

## FAMILY FOIL POTATOES — Page 65

3 to 4 med. sliced potatoes
1 small onion, sliced

1-10 3/4 oz. can of any cream soup

Place sliced potatoes on a large piece of heavy-duty aluminum foil, sprayed with nonstick cooking spray. Top with onion slices. Cover with soup and season as desired. Fold (see "Basic Hamburger Foil Dinner"). Cook for about 1 hour on the grill, over an open fire (turning about every 15 minutes), or in a *(Complete Recipe on page 65)*

# BASIC HAMBURGER FOIL DINNER

PER SERVING:

| | |
|---|---|
| I lg. hamburger patty | 2 carrots, sliced or sticks |
| (about 1/2 lb.) | 1 onion slice |
| 1 small potato, sliced | salt, pepper, garlic to taste |

Tear off large piece of heavy-duty aluminum foil. Spray with nonstick cooking spray. Place raw hamburger in center of foil and layer rest of ingredients on top. Put a pat of butter on top. Fold as instructed below. Repeat for each dinner. Cook for about 1 hour or until hamburger is done and vegetables are tender, turning occasionally to prevent burning. Can be grilled, cooked over the open fire, or baked in 350 degree oven.

FOLDING A FOIL DINNER: Fold long edges of foil together and fold over down to food. Roll other 2 ends up to food. Gently press top seam to seal. ALWAYS OPEN COOKED FOIL PACKETS CAREFULLY TO AVOID STEAM BURNS!

# FAMILY FOIL POTATOES

| | |
|---|---|
| 3 to 4 med. sliced potatoes | 1-10 3/4 oz. can of any cream soup |
| 1 small onion, sliced | |

Place sliced potatoes on a large piece of heavy-duty aluminum foil, sprayed with nonstick cooking spray. Top with onion slices. Cover with soup and season as desired. Fold (see "Basic Hamburger Foil Dinner"). Cook for about 1 hour on the grill, over an open fire (turning about every 15 minutes), or in a 350 degree oven, until potatoes are tender.

Suggested soup flavors: cream of mushroom, cream of celery, or cream of chicken. Use cheddar cheese soup for easy au gratin potatoes.

# HAM AND SWEET POTATO FOIL DINNER

PER SERVING:

| | |
|---|---|
| **1/2-1 C. large ham chunks** | **Brown sugar to taste** |
| **1 sweet potato, sliced** | **Pat of butter** |
| **1/2 C. pineapple chunks** | |

Place ham chunks on a large piece of heavy-duty aluminum foil, sprayed with nonstick cooking spray. Top with remaining ingredients. Fold (see "Basic Hamburger Foil Dinner"). Repeat for each dinner. Cook for about 1 hour on the grill, over an open fire (turning occasionally), or in a 350 degree oven, until sweet potatoes are tender.


# ORANGE ROUGHY FOIL DINNER

PER SERVING:

| | |
|---|---|
| **1-2 pieces of orange roughy** | **1/2 C. frozen mixed vegetables** |
| **1 small potato, sliced** | **Pat of butter** |

Place orange roughy on a large piece of heavy-duty aluminum foil, sprayed with nonstick cooking spray. Top with remaining ingredients, ending with pat of butter. Season as desired. Fold (see "Basic Hamburger Foil Dinner"). Repeat for each dinner. Cook for about 1 hour on the grill, over an open fire (turning occasionally), or in a 350 degree oven, until potato is tender.


# SHIPWRECK IN FOIL

PER SERVING:

| | |
|---|---|
| **1/4 lb. ground beef** | **1/2-14 oz. can kidney beans** |
| **1 small potato, sliced** | **1/2-10 3/4 oz. can tomato soup** |
| **2 slices of onion** | **Salt, pepper, garlic powder to taste** |

Place sliced potato on a large piece of heavy-duty aluminum foil, sprayed with nonstick cooking spray. Crumble raw ground beef over potato. Layer onion slices and kidney beans (drained) on top of ground beef. Spoon tomato soup over top and season. Fold (see "Basic Hamburger Foil Dinner"). Repeat for each dinner. Cook for about 1 hour on the grill, over an open fire (turning occasionally), or in a 350 degree oven, until beef is done and potato is tender.

# FRESH FISH IN FOIL

PER SERVING:

| | |
|---|---|
| 1 fresh water fish fillet (about 1/2 lb.) | 1/2 env. dry onion soup mix |
| 1-8 oz. can whole potatoes, drained and halved | 1-8 oz. can sliced carrots |
| | 1/4 C. water |

Place fish fillet on a large piece of heavy-duty aluminum foil, sprayed with nonstick cooking spray. Top fish with potatoes and carrots. Mix soup mix with water; pour evenly over vegetables. Fold (see "Basic Hamburger Foil Dinner"). Repeat for each dinner. Cook for about 20 minutes on the grill, over an open fire (turning occasionally), or in a 350 degree oven, or until fish flakes.

# KRAUT AND RIBS FOIL DINNER

PER SERVING:

| | |
|---|---|
| Spareribs | 1 small potato, sliced |
| 1/2-15 oz. can sauerkraut, drained | 2 onion slices |
| Pat of butter | |

Place spareribs on a large piece of heavy-duty aluminum foil, sprayed with nonstick cooking spray. Top with remaining ingredients, ending with a pat of butter. Fold (see "Basic Hamburger Foil Dinner"). Repeat for each dinner. Cook for about 1 hour on the grill, over an open fire (turning occasionally), or in a 350 degree oven, until ribs are done and potato is tender. A thin-sliced pork chop may be substituted for the ribs.

# BEEF STEW IN FOIL

PER SERVING:

| | |
|---|---|
| 1/4 lb. beef stew chunks | 1 slice bacon, cut in pieces |
| 1 small potato, cubed | 1 carrot, sliced |
| 1 tomato, quartered | 1/2 onion, sliced |

Place all ingredients on a large piece of heavy-duty aluminum foil, sprayed with nonstick cooking spray. Season as desired. Fold (see "Basic Hamburger Foil Dinner"). Repeat for each dinner. Cook for about 1 hour on the grill, over an open fire (turning occasionally), or in a 350 degree oven, until beef and vegetables are tender.

# SHRIMP BARBECUE

PER SERVING:
**4 to 5 large pieces of raw shrimp      1 T. butter**
**Garlic, salt, pepper, and parsley**
**   to taste**

Clean and peel shrimp.  Place shrimp on a large piece of heavy-duty aluminum foil, sprayed with nonstick cooking spray.  Cream butter with seasonings.  Top shrimp with butter mixture.  Fold (see "Basic Hamburger Foil Dinner").  Repeat for each dinner.  Cook 5 to 10 minutes on grill or over an open fire (turning occasionally), until shrimp is done.


# GINGER CHICKEN AND VEGETABLES

PER SERVING:
**1 boneless, skinless chicken         1/4 tsp. soy sauce**
**   breast, cut in 1/2" strips           1/4 tsp. ginger**
**1/2 C. small broccoli florets          1/2 tsp. olive oil**
**1/3 C. mushrooms, quartered       Hot, cooked rice**
**1/4 red pepper, cut in chunks**

Combine oil, soy sauce, and ginger.  Add chicken and vegetables and toss until evenly coated.  Place chicken mixture on a large piece of heavy-duty aluminum foil, sprayed with nonstick cooking spray.  Fold (see "Basic Hamburger Foil Dinner").  Repeat for each dinner.  Cook for about 15 to 20 minutes on the grill, over an open fire (turning occasionally), or in a 350 degree oven, until chicken is done.  Serve with rice.


# PIZZA TOMATOES

**4 med. tomatoes                          Basil**
**10 precooked sausage links         Mozzarella cheese slices**
**Oregano**

Slice tomatoes into thirds; place cut-side up on a piece of heavy-duty aluminum foil, sprayed with nonstick cooking spray.  Sprinkle lightly with oregano and basil.  Slice cooked sausage links and place on top of tomatoes.  Top with mozzarella cheese slices.  Seal foil lightly above cheese and grill for 15 to 20 minutes, or until cheese is melted

# CAMPFIRE POT ROAST

4 lbs. chuck roast
6 small carrots
2 med. onions, quartered

2 med. tomatoes, cut in wedges
1 green pepper, cut in wedges
Salt and pepper

Brown chuck roast on a greased grill; season with salt and pepper. Tear off a 5 ft. piece of aluminum foil and fold in half for strength; spray with nonstick cooking spray. Place meat in center of foil and cover with vegetables. Season with salt and pepper. Seal well and cook over coals for 1 1/2 to 2 hours.

# MUSHROOMS IN FOIL

Large, fresh whole mushrooms        Salad oil

Dip mushrooms in oil and place on a piece of heavy-duty aluminum foil, sprayed with nonstick cooking spray. Season as desired with salt and pepper. Seal foil and grill for about 15 minutes.

These mushrooms are also good using olive oil or red wine salad dressing.

# APPLE DELIGHT

PER SERVING:
1 apple
1 tsp. sugar
Cinnamon to taste

1 T. raisins
1 T. all-purpose baking mix

Core and chop apple in fairly large pieces, peeled if desired. Mix sugar, raisins, cinnamon, and baking mix together. Stir mixture into chopped apple. Wrap in a piece of heavy-duty aluminum foil, sprayed with nonstick cooking spray, leaving sufficient room for steam. Grill for about 30 to 45 minutes.

## SAUCY DOGS

1/2 lb. hot dogs
1/4 C. Cheddar cheese, shredded
1 hard-boiled egg, cut up
1/8 C. chili sauce

1 T. pickle relish
1/2 tsp. mustard
1/4 tsp. garlic salt
Hot dog buns

Chop hot dogs into small chunks. Add cheese to hot dogs. Add remaining ingredients, except buns, to hot dog mixture; mix well. Spread mixture on hot dog buns. Wrap in foil. Bake at 350 degrees or grill for 15 minutes.

Great way to use leftover hot dogs!

## BAKED BANANA

**1-2 bananas per serving**

Wrap banana (skin on) in a piece of heavy duty aluminum foil. Grill about 10 minutes.

## NOTES:

_____

_____

_____

_____

_____

_____

_____

# SOUP, SALADS AND SANDWICHES

## My Favorites

### STUFFED PEPPER SOUP

Page 73

3/4 C. instant rice
3/4 C. water
1 lb. ground beef
1-14.5 oz. can beef broth
Italian seasoning, garlic powder,
and pepper to taste

1-14 1/2 oz. can diced tomatoes
1-10 3/4 oz. can tomato soup
2 large green peppers (about 4 C.
chopped into large chunks)
1 medium onion

Chop green peppers and onion into large chunks. Boil water; remove water from heat, add instant rice, cover and set aside. Brown ground beef in a pot, adding green peppers and onions about halfway through
*(Complete Recipe on page 73)*

### TACO JOES

Page 82

1 lb. ground beef
1-10 3/4 oz. can tomato soup
Hamburger buns

1 C. thick and chunky salsa
Cheddar cheese, shredded

Brown ground beef; drain. Add tomato soup and salsa. Simmer for 5-10 minutes, stirring frequently. Serve on buns and sprinkle with Cheddar cheese. *(Recipe on page 82)*

# STUFFED PEPPER SOUP

3/4 C. instant rice
3/4 C. water
1 lb. ground beef
1-14.5 oz. can beef broth
Italian seasoning, garlic powder,
  and pepper to taste

1-14 1/2 oz. can diced tomatoes
1-10 3/4 oz. can tomato soup
2 large green peppers (about 4 C.
  chopped into large chunks)
1 medium onion

Chop green peppers and onion into large chunks. Boil water; remove water from heat, add instant rice, cover and set aside. Brown ground beef in a pot, adding green peppers and onions about halfway through cooking time; drain. Add beef broth, tomatoes (undrained), tomato soup, Italian seasoning, garlic powder, and pepper. Cover and simmer for 10 minutes. Add rice, cover and simmer for an additional 10 minutes.

For thinner soup, decrease rice and water to 1/2 C. each. For thicker soup, increase rice and water to 1 C. each. Serve as a soup or over mashed potatoes.


# HAMBURGER DUMP STEW

1 lb. ground beef
1-14 1/2 can stewed tomatoes
1-15 1/4 oz can whole kernel corn
1-14.5 oz. can sliced carrots
Salt, pepper, garlic powder to
  taste

1-10 3/4 oz. can tomato soup
1-14.5 oz. can diced potatoes
1-14.5 oz. can cut green beans
1-8 oz. jar pearl onions

Form ground beef into 4 patties about 1/2" thick. Place patties on a microwave plate and microwave on high for 3 to 5 minutes, until no longer pink. Patties can also be fried or grilled. Let patties cool. Cut patties into bite-size pieces. Dump meat and remaining ingredients into a large pot, including the liquids from the vegetables (for a thicker stew, drain just the potatoes). Season as desired with salt, pepper, and garlic powder. Bring to a boil; reduce heat and simmer for 5 to 10 minutes.

This is an excellent recipe for leftover hamburgers!

# CABBAGE AND BEEF SOUP

1 lb. ground beef
1/2 tsp. garlic salt
1/4 tsp. garlic powder
1/4 tsp. pepper
1-16 oz. can kidney beans,
    undrained
1/2 medium cabbage, chopped

2 tsp. beef bouillon
2 stalks celery, chopped
1-28 oz. can tomatoes, liquid
    reserved, chopped
1 tomato can of water

In a Dutch oven, brown beef; drain. Add remaining ingredients. Bring to a boil. Reduce heat and simmer covered for 1 hour.


# PIZZA LOVERS SOUP

1 lb. sausage, hot and spicy
4 oz. sliced pepperoni
1-26 oz. can tomato soup
2 soup cans of water
2 cups fresh tomatoes, chopped
1/2 medium onion, chopped
1/2 large green pepper, sliced thin

4 oz. fresh mushrooms, sliced
1 rounded T. dried basil
1 rounded T. dried oregano
1 rounded T. onion powder
1 rounded T. garlic powder
Mozzarella cheese to garnish

Brown sausage and drain well. Sauté onions, green pepper, and mushrooms over low heat (do not add oil or butter). Add sautéed vegetables and tomatoes to sausage. Put tomato soup in a pot and slowly add water, stirring to blend well. Add sausage mixture and remaining ingredients, except mozzarella cheese, to pot; mix well. Simmer over low heat at least 1 hour to combine flavors. Garnish each serving with mozzarella cheese.


# CREAMY POTATO SOUP

6 med. potatoes, cubed
1 C. small ham chunks (8 oz.)
1/2 med. onion, chopped
1 T. chicken bouillon

2 stalks celery, sliced
1 stick butter
1 C. milk

In a pot, melt butter. Add onions, celery, ham chunks, and chicken bouillon. Cook about 5 minutes or until vegetables are tender. Add potatoes and enough water to cover. Cook until potatoes are tender and soup is thick, adding additional water if necessary. Stir in milk.

# CREAM OF PARISIAN SOUP

1 lb. frozen cauliflower, carrots,
  and broccoli
1 stick butter
1/2 C. celery, chopped
1/2 C. onion, chopped

1 C. flour
9 tsp. chicken bouillon
6 C. milk
2 C. chopped ham

Cook cauliflower, carrots, and broccoli in 2 C. water, do not drain. Set aside. In a pot, sauté celery and onions in melted butter. Add flour, then add milk slowly. Stir in chicken bouillon. Stir over medium heat until thick and smooth. Add cooked vegetables with liquid and ham.

Diced chicken can be used in place of ham; or soup can be made without meat, if desired.


# CREAMY POTATO AND HAM CHOWDER

2 C. frozen hash browns with
  onions and green peppers
1-14 1/2 oz. can chicken broth
1 1/2 C. milk
2 T. cornstarch

4 oz. cream cheese
1 1/2 C. cooked ham, cubed
1/2 C. frozen whole-kernel
  corn
Cheddar cheese (optional)

Combine hash browns and broth in a large pot; bring to a boil. Reduce heat and simmer covered for 2 minutes. Combine milk and cornstarch; add to hash brown mixture along with cream cheese. Add ham and corn. Cook, stirring constantly, until thickened and bubbly. Cook an additional 2 minutes, stirring constantly. Garnish with cheese if desired.


# BROCCOLI CHEESE SOUP

1-10 oz. pkg. frozen broccoli
1 C. water
2 tsp. chicken bouillon

1 C. shredded Cheddar cheese
1/2 C. flour
1 C. milk

Thaw broccoli and chop. Mix water and chicken bouillon together; bring to a boil. Add broccoli to broth and cook until tender. Combine remaining ingredients and mix well; add broccoli and broth. Heat until thickened.

# TURKEY SOUP

1 C. cooked turkey, chopped
1 qt. chicken broth
1/4 C. onion, chopped
1/4 C. celery, chopped
Garlic powder, seasoned salt,
   pepper to taste

1 large potato, diced
4 carrots, chopped
1-14 oz. can diced tomatoes
   with green chilies
Cooked noodles

Mix all ingredients together except noodles, and cook about 1 to 2 hours until vegetables are tender. Add cooked noodles to desired thickness.


# EASY CHILI

2 lbs. ground beef
1 med. onion, chopped
1 green pepper, chopped
1-28 oz. can crushed tomatoes
1-15 1/2 oz. can chili beans
1-8 oz. can mushrooms, drained

1-15 oz. can seasoned tomato sauce
1-26 oz. can tomato soup
2 tsp. garlic powder
2 T. chili powder
2 tsp. pepper
2 tsp. seasoned salt

In a large pot, brown ground beef with onions and green peppers; drain. Add remaining ingredients. Simmer over low heat for 1 hour to combine flavors.

TIP: Leftover sloppy joe meat works well in this recipe in place of the ground beef.


# BEEF STEW

2 lb. beef stew meat
1 lg. onion, chopped
4 medium potatoes, cubed
3 carrots, sliced
1-1 1/2 oz. pkg. beef stew
   seasoning

1-46 oz. can tomato juice
2 tsp. minced garlic
1 T. pepper
1 tsp. seasoned salt
1 T. vegetable oil

Cook beef in a pot with oil until browned. Add remaining ingredients. Bring to a boil; reduce heat and simmer for 1 hour, until beef and vegetables are tender.

# CROCK POT ITALIAN CHICKEN STEW

3 boneless, skinless chicken
   breasts
1-28 oz. can tomatoes
1 lg. potato, cubed
1-14 1/2 oz. jar pearl onions
1 C. sliced carrots

2 T. tomato paste
1 tsp. minced garlic
1 T. sugar
1/2 tsp. ground red pepper
1/2 tsp. salt

Cut chicken into 1" pieces. Combine all ingredients in a 3 1/2 qt. crock pot. Cook on low 8 to 10 hours.

Excellent served over cooked pasta!


# MINESTRONE SOUP

1 lb. smoked Italian sausage
1 T. olive or vegetable oil
1 C. onion, chopped
1/2 tsp. minced garlic
1 C. carrots, sliced
1 tsp. dried basil
2 sm. zucchini, sliced (optional)

2-10 3/4 oz. cans beef broth
2 C. cabbage, finely chopped
1 tsp. salt
1/4 tsp. pepper
1-1 lb. jar Great Northern beans
   (undrained)

Slice sausage about 1/4" thick and brown in oil. Add remaining ingredients and cook slowly until all vegetables are tender. Add more broth (or water) to make sure vegetables remain covered during cooking.


# CUBED BEEF CHILI

2 lbs. stew meat
1-14 1/2 oz. can stewed tomatoes
1 tsp. sugar
Garlic powder, chili powder to taste

2-15 1/2 oz. chili beans
1-16 oz. jar salsa

Spray 3 1/2-qt. crock pot with nonstick cooking spray. Put raw stew meat in bottom of crock pot. Layer stewed tomatoes, chili beans, and salsa on top of beef. Sprinkle top with sugar, garlic powder, and chili powder. Cook on low 8 to 10 hours. Stir before serving.

Easy and delicious!

# BEAN AND MAC CHOWDER

1/2 C. onion, chopped
1/2 C. celery, chopped
1 tsp. minced garlic
1 T. vegetable oil
2 medium tomatoes, chopped
2-14 1/2 oz. cans chicken broth
1 3/4 C. water
1/2 tsp. oregano

1/2 tsp. basil
1/4 tsp. pepper
3-15 1/4 oz. cans Great
    Northern beans, rinsed and
    drained
1 C. uncooked elbow
    macaroni

In a large saucepan, sauté onion and celery in oil until tender. Add minced garlic and chopped tomato; simmer for 5 minutes. Add chicken broth, water, oregano, basil, and pepper. Bring to a boil over medium heat; cook for 5 minutes. Add beans and macaroni; return to a boil. Reduce heat; simmer, uncovered, for 15 minutes or until macaroni is tender.

Pinto beans (rinsed and drained) can be substituted for great northern beans. Try adding 1/2 lb. sliced, precooked smoked sausage, to soup for a great main dish!

# NEW ENGLAND CLAM CHOWDER

3 slices bacon, cut in pieces
3-6 1/2 oz. cans minced clams
2 C. potatoes, peeled and diced
1 medium onion, chopped
1/4 C. flour

2 C. milk
3/4 C. light cream
1 tsp. salt
1/8 tsp. pepper

Place cut bacon in a 2-qt. casserole dish. Microwave on high for 2 minutes. Drain clam liquid into bacon and drippings. Set clams aside. Stir potatoes and onion into bacon mixture. Cover and microwave on high for 8 minutes, or until vegetables are tender. Blend in flour until smooth. Stir in milk. Cover and microwave on power level "8" for 3 minutes. Stir in clams, cream, salt and pepper. Do not cover. Microwave on power level "8" for 3 minutes, or until hot.

## EASY TOMATO RAVIOLI SOUP

1-10 3/4 oz. can tomato soup
1 C. water

1-15 oz. can mini ravioli,
in tomato sauce

Put tomato soup into a saucepan. Slowly add water, stirring to blend well. Add ravioli and stir gently to blend. Cook over medium heat until hot.

Excellent served with grilled cheese sandwiches!

## SPAGHETTI SALAD

1 lb. spaghetti, cooked, drained,
and rinsed with cold water
8 oz. Italian salad dressing
4 T. salad seasoning

1 green pepper, chopped
1 cucumber, chopped
6 to 8 green onions, sliced
3 to 4 tomatoes, chopped

In a bowl, mix all ingredients together with hands or spaghetti server and chill. Additional salad dressing can be added if salad becomes too dry.

TIP: Break uncooked spaghetti in half or in thirds to make salad easier to eat.

## TACO SALAD

1 lb. ground beef
1-15 oz. can kidney beans,
undrained
3/4 pkg. taco seasoning
1/2 medium red onion
chopped

1 head of lettuce
1 pint cherry tomatoes
4 oz. Cheddar cheese, shredded
8 oz. Thousand Island salad
dressing
5 to 7 oz. broken tortilla chips

Brown ground beef; drain. Add undrained kidney beans and taco seasoning; simmer 10 minutes and set aside to cool. Break lettuce into bite-size pieces. Toss lettuce with onion and cherry tomatoes; then with salad dressing. Add cooled beef mixture, cheese, and tortilla chips, mixing gently.

Western salad dressing can be used in place of Thousand Island, if desired.

# GARBANZO CUCUMBER SALAD

1-15 oz. can garbanzo beans,
   rinsed and drained
1 medium cucumber, sliced and
   quartered
Red wine-vinegar salad dressing

1/2 C. sliced black olives
1/3 C. red onion, chopped
1/4 C. fresh parsley

In a bowl, combine beans, cucumber, olives, onion, and parsley. Toss with salad dressing to taste (about 6 to 8 T.). Serve immediately or chill up to 24 hours.

# LAYERED SALAD

Lettuce, about 1/2 head
1 C. celery, chopped
1/2 C. onion, chopped
1-8 oz. can waterchestnuts,
   sliced and drained
2-10 oz. pkgs. frozen peas,
   unthawed

4 hard-boiled eggs
3 C. Miracle Whip Salad Dressing
3 T. sugar
2 C. Cheddar cheese, shredded
1 pint cherry tomatoes
Bacon bits

Break lettuce into bite-size pieces and make about a 1" layer in a 9x13" plastic container. Sprinkle celery over lettuce. Sprinkle onions over celery. Sprinkle waterchestnuts over onions. Sprinkle frozen peas over waterchestnuts. Slice eggs and place over peas. Mix salad dressing and sugar together; gently spread mixture over eggs. Cover with cheese. Cut cherry tomatoes in half and place on top of cheese, cut side down. Sprinkle with bacon bits to color. Cover and chill 8 to 12 hours or overnight.

IMPORTANT: Do not thaw peas before using in this recipe. Do not use real mayonnaise. This recipe can also be layered as above in a bowl; or can be cut in half and layered in a 9" square plastic container.

# TUNA-MAC SALAD

| | |
|---|---|
| 2 C. uncooked elbow macaroni | 1 1/2 C. mayonnaise |
| 2 stalks celery, sliced | 1 T. sugar |
| 1/4 C. onions, chopped | 1 T. vinegar |
| 1-12 oz. can tuna, drained | 1/2 tsp. salt |

Cook macaroni as directed on pkg.; drain and rinse under cold water. Mix mayonnaise, sugar, vinegar, and salt. Combine mayonnaise mixture with macaroni, celery, onions, and tuna. Chill.

If desired, 1 C. cooked, cooled peas can be added to above recipe.

# QUICK TACO SALAD

| | |
|---|---|
| 1-16 oz. can chili beans, undrained | 1 tomato, chopped |
| 5 oz. corn chips | 1/2 sm. onion, chopped |
| 1 C. Cheddar cheese, shredded | 1/2 C. salsa |
| 2 C. shredded lettuce | 1/4 C. sour cream |
| 1-2 1/4 oz. can sliced black olives | |

Heat the chili beans in a saucepan or microwave. Place corn chips on a plate. Top with beans, cheese, lettuce, tomatoes, onion, salsa, sour cream, and olives (drained). Serve immediately.

# THREE BEAN SALAD

| | |
|---|---|
| 1-15 oz. can yellow wax beans | 1/3 C. oil |
| 1-15 oz. can green beans | 3/4 C. sugar |
| 1-15 oz. can red beans | 2/3 C. vinegar |
| 1 large green pepper, chopped | 1/2 tsp. salt |
| 2 med. onion, cut in fine rings | |

Drain all beans and put in a bowl; add green peppers and onion. Combine oil, sugar, vinegar, and salt. Heat oil mixture and pour over beans. Chill for about 8 hours, stirring often.

# HOT CHICKEN SALAD

3 C. chicken, cooked and
  chopped
1 1/2 C. celery, chopped
1/2 C. slivered almonds
1-8 oz. can sliced waterchestnuts,
  drained

1 C. mayonnaise
1 1/2 C. Cheddar cheese,
  shredded
1 1/2 C. crushed potato chips

Mix together chicken, celery, almonds, waterchestnuts, and mayonnaise. Put into a casserole dish. Cover with cheese and top with potato chips. Bake at 375 degrees for 25 minutes.


# TACO JOES

1 lb. ground beef
1-10 3/4 oz. can tomato soup
Hamburger buns

1 C. thick and chunky salsa
Cheddar cheese, shredded

Brown ground beef; drain. Add tomato soup and salsa. Simmer for 5-10 minutes, stirring frequently. Serve on buns and sprinkle with Cheddar cheese.


# CLUB SANDWICH DELUXE

FOR EACH SANDWICH:
2 slices of bread
2 slices of cheese
1 slice of ham
Pickle slices
1/4 C. sauerkraut, drained well

3 slices of bacon, cooked
Lettuce
Tomato slice
Mayonnaise
Mustard

Make a sauce, using mayonnaise and mustard to taste. Spread sauce on both slices of bread. Layer the following on bread: 1 slice of cheese, ham, pickles, sauerkraut, bacon, lettuce, tomato, and another slice of cheese.

This sandwich is a meal in itself!

# OPEN-FACE VEGETABLE SANDWICH

FOR EACH SANDWICH:

| | |
|---|---|
| **1 slice of toast** | **1 slice of tomato** |
| **1 C. cole slaw** | **1 slice of American cheese** |

Place slice of toast on a microwave-safe plate. Place cole slaw on top of toast. Put slice of tomato on top of cole slaw and top with slice of cheese. Cook in microwave on high just until cheese is melted. Serve with fresh fruit if desired.

Recipe can also be made with chicken salad or tuna salad in place of cole slaw.

# CHICKEN JOES

| | |
|---|---|
| **1-11 oz. can chicken** | **1-6 oz. box chicken-flavored stuffing** |
| **1-10 3/4 oz. can cream of** | **mix (with seasoning packet)** |
| **chicken soup** | **1-15 oz. can chicken broth** |
| **Buns or biscuits** | |

In a 3 1/2-qt. crock pot, combine chicken, soup, stuffing mix (with seasoning), and broth. Cook on low until heated throughout. Serve on buns or over biscuits.

# BUNSTEADS

| | |
|---|---|
| **1-7 oz. can chicken or tuna** | **2 T. onion, chopped** |
| **1 C. Cheddar cheese, cubed** | **2 T. green olives, chopped** |
| **3 eggs, hard-boiled and chopped** | **2 T. sweet relish** |
| **2 T. green pepper, chopped** | **1/2 C. mayonnaise** |
| **6 hamburger buns** | |

Combine all ingredients except buns; mix lightly. Divide and spread mixture on buns; wrap individually in aluminum foil. Bake at 250 degrees for about 30 minutes or until heated and cheese is melted.

TIP: Sandwiches can be made ahead of time and wrapped in foil. Sandwiches can also be heated on a grill instead of the oven. If desired, shredded cheese can be used instead of cubed cheese.

# BBQ BACON CHEESEBURGERS

| | |
|---|---|
| 1 1/2 lb. ground beef | 4 onion slices |
| 8 slices bacon, cooked | Barbecue sauce |
| 4 slices American cheese | 4 hamburger buns |

Divide ground beef and form 4 patties. Fry or grill patties until no longer pink; top with cheese slices and continue cooking until cheese is melted. Drain on paper towels. Place patties on buns and top with bacon slices, onion slices, and barbecue sauce to taste.

Great way to use leftover bacon!


# TURKEY SALADWICHES

| | |
|---|---|
| 2 1/2 C. turkey, cooked and diced | 1/8 C. green pepper, chopped |
| 3/4 C. celery, finely chopped | 1/8 C. onion, chopped |
| 6 hard rolls, halved lengthwise | 2/3 C. mayonnaise |

Combine turkey, celery, green pepper, and onion; stir in mayonnaise. Chill. Scoop out centers of rolls to make slightly hollow; toast lightly in oven or over grill. Fill each half with turkey mixture.

———————

# NOTES:

_____

_____

_____

_____

_____

_____

_____

# VEGETABLES
# AND
# SIDE DISHES

## My Favorites

Page 90

### BBQ SAUERKRAUT

1 C. brown sugar
1-28 oz. can sauerkraut

1 lb. ground beef
1-28 oz. can tomato sauce

Brown ground beef. Meanwhile, drain sauerkraut and rinse.
Mix all ingredients together and put in a 3-qt. casserole dish.
Bake uncovered at 350 degrees for 1 hour.

Page 92

### CORN SPOON BREAD

1 stick butter, softened
1-8 1/2 oz. box cornbread mix

1-14 oz. can whole kernel corn
1-14 oz. can cream style corn
8 oz. sour cream
2 eggs

Mix all ingredients together and put in a 3-qt. casserole dish,
sprayed with nonstick cooking spray. Bake at 350 degrees
for 30 minutes or until hot and bubbly.
*(Complete Recipe on page 92)*

# CROCK POT

## CROCK POT MASHED POTATOES

(crock pot)

8 lg. potatoes (12 C. cooked
  and mashed)
2-3 oz. pkgs. cream cheese,
  softened
1 C. sour cream

1-1 oz. env. Ranch dressing
  mix
1 stick butter, softened
2 tsp. parsley flakes

Peel, dice, and cook potatoes until tender. Mash with a potato masher; potatoes will be thick. In a large bowl, combine cream cheese, sour cream, butter, salad dressing mix, and parsley. Stir in potatoes. For creamier potatoes, whip potatoes with a mixer. Transfer to a 4-qt. crock pot. Cover and cook on low 2 to 4 hours.

TIP: A 4-qt. Dutch oven generously filled with large, raw potato chunks makes about 12 C. cooked, mashed potatoes. Makes an excellent potluck dish, since potatoes stay warm in the crock pot!

# MICROWAVE

## RICE AND MUSHROOMS

(microwave)

1 1/2 C. instant rice
1 1/2 C. hot water
1/4 C. butter
1/4 C. onion, chopped
1-4 oz. can mushrooms
1/2 cup frozen peas

1/4 tsp. garlic powder
2 tsp. beef bouillon
1/4 tsp. basil
2 T. parsley
Parmesan cheese

Mix all ingredients, except Parmesan cheese, together. Put into a 2-qt. casserole dish, sprayed with nonstick cooking spray. Sprinkle lightly with Parmesan cheese. Microwave on high for 7 minutes.

## BROCCOLI CHEESE POTATO TOPPER

(microwave)

1-10 3/4 oz. can Cheddar cheese
  soup
2 T. sour cream
Baked potatoes

1/2 tsp. Dijon mustard
1 C. broccoli flowerets,
  cooked and drained

In a microwave-safe bowl, combine soup, sour cream, and Dijon mustard. Microwave on high 2 1/2 minutes, stirring once. Stir in broccoli and microwave for 1 minute. Spoon over baked potatoes.

## OVEN

## BROCCOLI AND CHEESE

(oven)

2-10 oz. pkgs. frozen broccoli
1 1/2 C. instant rice (uncooked)
1 stick butter
1 medium onion, chopped
1-4 oz. can sliced mushrooms,
  drained

1-10 3/4 oz. can cream of mushroom
  soup
1-10 3/4 oz. can Cheddar cheese
  soup

Sauté onion in butter. Mix in cream of mushroom soup and Cheddar cheese soup. Add broccoli and rice; stir well. Put in 3-qt. casserole dish, sprayed with nonstick cooking spray. Sprinkle mushrooms on top. Cover and bake at 350 degrees for 45 minutes.

## CORN AND BROCCOLI BAKE

(oven)

1-14 oz. can cream corn
1-10 oz. pkg. frozen broccoli
1/2 C. crushed saltine crackers,
  divided

1 egg, beaten
1 T. dried onion
2 T. butter, softened

Combine corn, broccoli, 1/4 C. cracker crumbs, egg, and onion. Add a dash of pepper if desired. Put in a 1 1/2-qt. casserole dish. Combine butter and remaining cracker crumbs and sprinkle on top. Cover and bake at 350 degrees for 45 minutes.

# HAMBURGER BEAN BAKE (oven)

1 1/2 lb. ground beef
1 lb. bacon
1 C. onion, chopped
1/4 C. dark molasses
1/3 C. brown sugar
1/2 C. ketchup
1/2 tsp. minced garlic
1 T. vinegar

1 1/2 tsp. dry mustard
1 1/2 tsp. salt
1-28 oz. can pork and beans
1-15.5 oz. can kidney beans
1-15.5 oz. can lima beans
1-15.5 oz. can yellow beans
1-15.5 oz. can green beans

Fry bacon, drain, and set aside. Brown ground beef and add onions shortly before meat is done. Drain all beans EXCEPT pork and beans, and rinse with water. Combine all ingredients, breaking bacon into bite-size pieces, and put into a 9x13" pan. Bake at 350 degrees for 1 hour.

It is very important not to drain the pork and beans. Any combination of your favorite beans can be used. This recipe makes an excellent potluck dish!


# HASH BROWN CHILI CHEESE PIE (oven)

1-6 oz. pkg. hash brown potato
  mix with onions
4 C. very hot water
2 T. butter
1 egg, slightly beaten
2 C. Colby-Monterey Jack cheese,
  shredded
2 sm. jalapeno chilies, seeded
  and finely chopped

1 small red bell pepper,
  finely chopped
2 T. flour
1/2 tsp. salt
2 eggs
2/3 C. milk
Shredded lettuce (optional)
Salsa (optional)
Sour cream (optional)

Cover hash browns with hot water. Let stand 15 minutes; drain thoroughly. Toss hash browns, butter, and 1 beaten egg. Press potato mixture on bottom and up sides of an ungreased 10" pie pan. Bake at 375 degrees for 20 minutes. Reduce oven heat to 350 degrees. Sprinkle half of the cheese, chilies, and bell pepper in the potato crust. Beat flour, salt, and 2 eggs until blended; stir in milk. Pour over cheese mixture. Bake at 350 degrees for 30 to 35 minutes or until center is set and top is golden brown. Let stand 10 minutes before cutting. Garnish with lettuce, salsa, and sour cream as desired.

# BBQ SAUERKRAUT (oven)

1 lb. ground beef
1-28 oz. can tomato sauce
1 C. brown sugar
1-28 oz. can sauerkraut

Brown ground beef. Meanwhile, drain sauerkraut and rinse. Mix all ingredients together and put in a 3-qt. casserole dish. Bake uncovered at 350 degrees for 1 hour.


# SWEET POTATO CASSEROLE (oven)

3 C. canned yams
1/2 C. butter
1 C. white sugar
1 tsp. vanilla

TOPPING:
1 C. brown sugar
1 C. finely chopped nuts
1/3 C. flour
1/3 C. butter, softened

Drain yams and mash. Add butter, white sugar, and vanilla. Mix and pour into a 2-qt casserole dish, sprayed with nonstick cooking spray. Mix ingredients for topping and sprinkle over yams. Bake at 350 degrees for 30 minutes or until golden brown.


# VEGETABLE PIZZA (oven)

1 pkg. crescent rolls
1/2 pkg. Ranch dressing mix
1/2 C. mayonnaise
Sliced radishes, mushrooms, green peppers and carrots to color
1-8 oz. pkg. cream cheese, softened
1/2 C. chopped cauliflower
1/2 C. chopped broccoli

Unroll crescent rolls and spread evenly on a pizza pan. Bake at 300 degrees for 10 minutes or until lightly browned. Cool completely. Mix ranch dressing mix, mayonnaise, and softened cream cheese. Spread on crust. Mix broccoli and cauliflower pieces and sprinkle over pizza. Sprinkle rest of vegetables enough to give pizza some color. Gently press vegetables into cream cheese mixture. Chill. Cut into wedges or squares to serve.

# CHEESE POTATOES

(oven)

5 large potatoes, cooked and
  diced
1-10 3/4 oz. can cream of chicken
  soup

1 1/2 C. Cheddar cheese, shredded
1/2 stick butter
8 oz. sour cream

Mix all ingredients together and put mixture into a casserole dish. Bake at 350 degrees for 30 minutes

# PIZZA POTATOES

(oven)

1-7.6 oz. pkg. scalloped potatoes
  mix
1-16 oz. can diced tomatoes
1 1/2 C. water
1/4 tsp. oregano

1-4 oz. pkg. sliced pepperoni
4 oz. mozzarella cheese,
  shredded

Empty potato slices and packet of seasoned sauce mix into 2-qt. casserole. In a saucepan, combine tomatoes, water, and oregano; heat to boiling; stir into potatoes. Arrange pepperoni on top and sprinkle with cheese. Bake uncovered at 375 degrees 30 to 35 minutes or until potatoes are tender.

VARIATION: Substitute 1/2 lb. ground beef or sausage, browned and drained, for pepperoni; stir into potato mixture.

# THREE CHEESE NOODLE BAKE

(oven)

2 C. uncooked noodles
1 C. cottage cheese
3/4 C. Cheddar cheese, shredded
1/2 C. sour cream
1/3 C. green onions, sliced

3 T. Parmesan cheese
1/2 tsp. Worcestershire sauce
1/8 tsp. pepper
2 eggs

Spray a 9x9" pan with nonstick cooking spray. Cook noodles according to pkg. directions; drain. Mix noodles and remaining ingredients. Spread in pan. Bake uncovered at 350 degrees for 30 to 35 minutes, or until center is set and edges are golden brown. Let stand 5 minutes before serving.

## CORN SPOON BREAD                              (oven)

1-14 oz. can whole kernel corn     1 stick butter, softened
1-14 oz. can cream style corn      1-8 1/2 oz. box cornbread mix
8 oz. sour cream                   2 eggs

Mix all ingredients together and put in a 3-qt. casserole dish, sprayed
with nonstick cooking spray. Bake at 350 degrees for 30 minutes or
until hot and bubbly.


# REFRIGERATOR


## MARINATED VEGETABLES                      (refrigerator)

2 T. vegetable oil                 1/4 tsp. pepper
2 T. white vinegar                 3 cucumbers, sliced
2 tsp. sugar                       3 fresh tomatoes, chopped
1/2 tsp. minced garlic             1 medium onion, sliced thin
1/4 tsp. salt

In a bowl, whisk oil, vinegar, sugar, garlic, salt and pepper. Add
cucumbers, chopped tomatoes, and onion; toss to coat. Cover and
refrigerate at least 1 hour or up to 6 hours.


# SKILLET


## BACON 'N BEANS                                (skillet)

1 lb. bacon                        1-3 lb. jar Great Northern beans
3 medium onions, sliced            2 green peppers, sliced in strips
3/4 C. brown sugar                 1-14 oz. can tomatoes
2 tsp. salt                        1/2 tsp. pepper

Cook bacon until crisp; cool and crumble. Add onion to bacon drippings
and cook until rings separate. Add green peppers and cook mixture
until onions are transparent. Add brown sugar. Drain beans and add
beans, tomatoes, salt and pepper, and bacon. Simmer for 40 minutes.

# CHINESE NOODLE TOSS

(skillet)

I/2 lb. multicolored noodles,
   cooked and drained
1 green pepper, sliced in strips
1/4 lb. fresh mushrooms, sliced
1 bunch green onions, sliced

4 slices bacon
1/2 tsp. minced garlic
1/2 tsp. ginger
1/8 C. soy sauce

Brown bacon until crisp; crumble. Add remaining ingredients except noodles; stir well. Add mixture to noodles and toss.

# SWEET AND SOUR CABBAGE

(skillet)

3 C. cabbage, shredded
1 medium green pepper, chopped
1 small onion, chopped
1/4 C. vinegar

1/4 C. sugar
1/2 tsp. celery seed
1/4 tsp. salt

Combine all ingredients and cook in a skillet until cabbage, green pepper, and onions are tender.

# SPAGHETTI CABBAGE FRY

(skillet)

1/2 small cabbage, chopped fine
8 oz. spaghetti
Salt and pepper to taste

1/2 medium onion, chopped
1/4 C. butter
1/4 tsp. minced garlic

In skillet, melt butter. Stir in cabbage, onion, and garlic. Cook, stirring occasionally, until cabbage is tender. Meanwhile, prepare spaghetti according to pkg. directions and drain. Toss hot spaghetti with cabbage mixture. Season as desired with salt and pepper.

TIP: Spaghetti can be cooked and drained ahead of time. Store in plastic storage bags. When ready to use, soak in hot water for about 5 minutes and drain. Spaghetti can also be frozen and used at a later date.

# WILTED LETTUCE SALAD　　　　　　　　(skillet)

Lettuce (about 1/2 head)　　　1 T. salt
1 medium onion, chopped　　　1 tsp. pepper
6 slices of bacon, cut up　　　1 tsp. garlic powder
1 C. vinegar　　　　　　　　　1/2 tsp. dry mustard
1/4 C. sugar

Tear up lettuce into a salad bowl. Fry bacon pieces until fairly well done. Remove bacon from skillet, drain, and put bacon into lettuce. Sauté onion in skillet for about 1 minute and remove from heat. Add vinegar, sugar, salt, pepper, garlic powder, and dry mustard to onion in skillet. Put back on heat and bring to a boil. Pour over lettuce and toss. Best served immediately.

---

## NOTES:

# DESSERTS

# My Favorites

**Page 105**

## PINEAPPLE WHIP

1-20 oz. can crushed pineapple, drained
1-14 oz. can sweetened, condensed milk

1/4 C. lemon juice
1/2 C. chopped nuts
1-12 oz. frozen whipped topping, thawed

Mix pineapple, lemon juice, and sweetened condensed milk in a bowl. Fold in whipped topping and nuts. Chill for 5 to 6 hours. *(Recipe on page 105)*

**Page 97**

## ANGEL CHOCOLATE DESSERT

1-5.9 oz. pkg. instant chocolate pudding mix
3 C. cold milk

1/4 to 1/2 angel food cake
8 oz. frozen whipped topping, thawed, divided

Cut angel food cake into bite-size pieces and put in bottom of an 8x8" plastic container, using enough cake to cover the bottom. Mix chocolate pudding and milk in a bowl according to pkg. directions. Let sit for 5 minutes to thicken. Stir in 4 oz. of thawed whipped *(Complete Recipe on page 97)*

# ICE CREAM SANDWICH DESSERT

**12-3 oz. neopolitan ice cream
  sandwiches
1-8 oz. frozen whipped
  topping**

**1 cup chopped malted milk
  balls (or favorite candy)**

Thaw whipped topping. Combine whipped topping and candy chunks. Put 2 layers of ice cream sandwiches in bottom of an 8x8" plastic container, cutting sandwiches as necessary. Spread whipped topping mixture over top of sandwiches. Freeze.

TIP: To chop candy, put in a plastic storage bag and pound lightly with a hammer. For easy cleanup, gently mix candy into container of whipped topping.


# ANGEL CHOCOLATE DESSERT

**1-5.9 oz. pkg. instant chocolate
  pudding mix
3 C. cold milk**

**1/4 to 1/2 angel food cake
8 oz. frozen whipped topping,
  thawed, divided**

Cut angel food cake into bite-size pieces and put in bottom of an 8x8" plastic container, using enough cake to cover the bottom. Mix chocolate pudding and milk in a bowl according to pkg. directions. Let sit for 5 minutes to thicken. Stir in 4 oz. of thawed whipped topping to pudding. Pour pudding mixture over cake cubes and spread evenly. Drop remaining whipped topping by spoonfuls over pudding and gently spread evenly. Cover and refrigerate for at least 4 to 5 hours.


# LIME CHEESECAKE

**1-8 oz. pkg. cream cheese,
  softened
1-14 oz. can sweetened
  condensed milk
3 tsp. vanilla**

**1/4 C. lime juice
Green food coloring
Graham cracker pie crust**

Combine cream cheese, sweetened condensed milk, vanilla, and lime juice. Add green food coloring as desired. Pour into graham cracker pie crust and freeze. Store in freezer.

# FAVORITE CHERRY CHEESECAKE

1 graham cracker pie crust
8 oz. frozen whipped topping,
  thawed

1-8 oz. pkg. cream cheese, softened
1-16 oz. can cherry pie filling

Put thawed whipped topping in a mixing bowl. Cut softened cream cheese into cubes and add to whipped topping. Mix with a hand mixer until fairly smooth (2 to 3 minutes). Spoon mixture into the graham cracker pie crust and smooth out evenly with back of spoon. Gently top with cherry pie filling. Refrigerate 2 to 3 hours before serving.

Any flavor of pie filling can be used in this recipe—try peach or blueberry!


# PUMPKIN WHIP

1-3.4 oz. pkg. instant
  butterscotch pudding mix
1 1/2 C. cold milk
1 C. canned pumpkin

1 tsp. pumpkin pie spice
1 1/2 C. frozen whipped
  topping, thawed

In a mixing bowl, beat pudding and milk until well blended, about 1 to 2 minutes. Blend in pumpkin and pie spice. Fold in whipped topping. Chill. Serve with gingersnaps or vanilla wafers if desired.


# CHEESECAKE PIE

1-8 oz. pkg. cream cheese,
  softened
1/3 C. sugar
2 tsp. vanilla
Assorted fresh fruit

8 oz. frozen whipped
  topping,  thawed
1 graham cracker pie crust

Beat cream cheese, sugar, and vanilla until smooth. Fold in whipped topping. Spoon mixture into crust. Chill until set, about 4 hours. Before serving, arrange fruit on top of filling.

VARIATION: For cheesecake snacks, spread filling on graham crackers and garnish with fruit.

# APPLE CRISP

4 tart cooking apples (about 4 C.)      1/3 C. butter, softened
2/3 C. packed brown sugar               3/4 tsp. cinnamon
1/2 C. flour                            3/4 tsp. nutmeg
1/2 C. instant or old-fashioned
   oats

Spray a 8" or 9" round or square pan with nonstick cooking spray.
Peel apples, if desired, and slice. Spread apples in pan. Mix brown
sugar, flour, oats, butter, cinnamon, and nutmeg with a fork until
crumbly. Sprinkle over apples. Bake at 375 degrees for 30 minutes
or until topping is golden brown and apples are tender. Serve with
milk or ice cream, if desired.


# ROCKY ROAD PIE

1 1/2 C. cold light cream               1/3 C. semi-sweet chocolate chips
1-3.4 oz. pkg. chocolate instant        1/3 C. miniature marshmallows
   pudding mix                          1/3 C. chopped nuts
8 oz. frozen whipped topping,           1 graham cracker pie shell
   thawed

Pour cold cream into a mixing bowl. Add pudding mix. Beat with a
wire whisk until well blended, about 1 minute. Let stand 5 minutes.
Fold in whipped topping, chocolate chips, marshmallows, and nuts.
Spoon into crust. Freeze until firm, about 6 hours or overnight. Remove
from freezer and let stand 10 minutes to soften before serving. Store
leftovers in the freezer.


# STRAWBERRY ICE CREAM PIE

1-10 oz. pkg. frozen strawberries       1 baked 8" or 9" pie crust
1-3 oz. pkg. strawberry gelatin         1 C. frozen whipped
1 pint vanilla ice cream                   topping, thawed

Thaw and drain strawberries, measuring syrup. Add enough water to
syrup to make 1 C.; bring to a boil. Remove from heat and stir in
gelatin until dissolved. Add ice cream by spoonfuls, stirring until melted.
Chill until thickened, about 10 minutes. Fold in strawberries. Pour
into cooled pie crust. Chill until firm, at least one hour. Garnish with
whipped topping.

# EASY BAVARIAN

1-3 oz. pkg. strawberry gelatin
1/4 C. sugar
1 C. boiling water

1 C. cold water
1 1/2 C. frozen whipped
   topping, thawed

Dissolve gelatin and sugar in 1 C. boiling water; stir until completely dissolved. Add 1 C. cold water. Chill until slightly thickened. Blend in whipped topping. Chill until firm. Garnish with additional whipped topping and fresh fruit if desired.


# MINI CHEESECAKES

12 vanilla wafers
2-8 oz. pkg. cream cheese,
   softened
Canned pie filling

1/2 C. sugar
1 tsp. vanilla
2 eggs

Line muffin tins with 12 foil liners. Place one vanilla wafer in each liner. Combine cream cheese, vanilla, and sugar with a hand mixer on medium speed until well-blended. Add eggs. Mix well. Pour over wafers, filling about 3/4 full. Bake at 325 degrees for 25 minutes. Remove from pan when cooled. Chill. Top each cheesecake with a spoonful of pie filling.

Cheesecakes can be garnished with fresh fruit, preserves, nuts or chocolate in place of pie filling, if desired.


# CHERRY MARSHMALLOW DESSERT

2-3 oz. pkgs. cherry gelatin
3 bananas, sliced
2 C. miniature marshmallows

1 C. sour cream
1/2 C. chopped nuts

Prepare gelatin as directed on pkg. Chill until almost firm. Fold in bananas. Pour into 8" square plastic container. Chill until firm. Combine marshmallows and sour cream; spread on top of gelatin. Top with chopped nuts. Chill.

Any fruit can be added to gelatin in place of, or with bananas.

# FROZEN CHOCOLATE-COVERED BANANAS

**2 bananas**
**10 toothpicks**
**1/3 C. semi-sweet chocolate chips**

**1/3 C. chocolate frosting**
**1 tsp. candy sprinkles (optional)**

Line a plate with waxed paper. Peel bananas and cut each into 5 chunks. Place bananas, cut side down, on waxed paper and insert a toothpick into each piece. Place plate in freezer for about 20 minutes or until bananas are frozen. Meanwhile, place chocolate chips in a small bowl and microwave on high for 60 to 90 seconds or until melted; stir. Add frosting and mix well. Microwave on high for 15 to 20 seconds or until of dipping consistency. Dip each banana chunk in chocolate mixture, spooning chocolate onto sides of banana chunks. Sprinkle with candy sprinkles if desired. Freeze dipped banana chunks for about 1 hour or until chocolate is firm and bananas are frozen.

TIP: If chocolate mixture becomes too stiff to dip, microwave on high for 5 to 10 seconds or until softened.


# FRUIT COCKTAIL PIE

**1-30 oz. can fruit cocktail,**
  **drained well**
**16 oz. sour cream**

**1/2 tsp. vanilla**
**1/4 C. sugar**
**1 graham cracker pie shell**

Mix drained fruit cocktail, sour cream, vanilla, and sugar in a bowl. Pour into graham cracker pie crust. Bake at 350 degrees for 20 minutes. Chill.


# EASY FRUIT COCKTAIL DESSERT

**1-30 oz. can fruit cocktail**
**16 oz. sour cream**

**4 C. miniature marshmallows**

Drain fruit cocktail. Mix all ingredients together. Chill 2 to 3 hours before serving.

# FRUIT COCKTAIL TORTE

1-16 oz. can fruit cocktail, drained
3/4 C. sugar
1 egg
1 C. flour

1 tsp. baking soda
1/4 tsp. salt
1/2 C. packed brown sugar
1/2 C. chopped nuts

In a bowl, combine white sugar and egg; beat well. Stir in fruit cocktail, flour, soda, and salt until mixed. Spread in a 8x8" microwave-safe pan. Combine brown sugar and nuts; sprinkle over top. Microwave on high for 8 to 10 minutes or until top springs back when lightly touched.

TIP: If your microwave does not have a turn-table, rotate dish after 5 minutes.


# DESSERT PIZZA

1-20 oz. pkg. refrigerated cookie dough, any flavor
3 C. frozen whipped topping, thawed

2 C. assorted fruit such as strawberries, grapes, peach slices, pineapple tidbits

Press cookie dough into 12" pizza pan. Bake 15 to 20 minutes or until golden brown. Cool in pan on wire rack. Place cookie crust on a serving plate if desired. Spread thawed whipped topping on crust. Garnish with fruit. Serve immediately or refrigerate until ready to serve.


# ORANGE SHERBERT BAVARIAN

1-3 oz. pkg. orange gelatin
1 C. boiling water
1 C. orange sherbert, softened

1/2 C. mandarin oranges, drained
1/2 C. crushed pineapple, drained
1/2 C. whipped cream

Add boiling water to gelatin and stir well to completely dissolve. Chill until slightly thickened. Whip with electric beater until fluffy. Fold in whipped cream, softened sherbert, mandarin oranges, and pineapple. Chill about 6 hours.

# EASY S'MORES

**Graham crackers, broken in half**    **Large marshmallows**
**Chocolate frosting**

For each s'more, spread one half of graham cracker with chocolate frosting. Heat marshmallow, on a long fork or stick, over an open fire until lightly browned. Place marshmallow on top of chocolate; then top with the other half of graham cracker. Squeeze gently and enjoy!

VARIATION: Spread one half of graham cracker with chocolate frosting and the other half with marshmallow cream. Put halves together, wrap in foil, and grill until chocolate is melted.


# TING-A-LINGS

**1-6 oz. pkg. semi-sweet**    **1-4 oz. can chow mein noodles**
   **chocolate chips**                **1 C. cashews**
**1-6 oz. pkg. butterscotch chips**

In a bowl in the microwave or in a sauce pan, melt chocolate and butterscotch chips. Remove from heat and add remaining ingredients. Drop by spoonfuls on waxed paper and let cool.


# ORANGE SHERBERT DESSERT

**1-3 oz. pkg. orange gelatin**    **1 C. mandarin oranges, drained**
**1 1/4 C. boiling water**          **8 oz. pineapple chunks**
**1/2 pint orange sherbert**       **1 banana, sliced**

Add gelatin to boiling water; stir until completely dissolved. Add orange sherbert; stir until blended. Let sit until mixture starts to thicken. Fold in mandarin oranges, pineapple chunks, and banana. Chill until thickened.

# ROCKY ROAD SQUARES

**4-4 1/2 oz. chocolate candy bars**    **3 C. miniature marshmallows**
**3/4 C. walnut pieces**

Melt chocolate in a bowl over hot water. Stir until smooth. Stir in marshmallows and walnuts. Spread mixture in a 8x8" pan, sprayed with nonstick cooking spray. Chill. Cut into squares to serve.


# FUDGE CICLES

**1-3.4 oz. pkg. instant chocolate**    **2 1/2 C. cold milk**
   **pudding mix**

Mix pudding and milk according to pkg. directions. Pour into ice cube trays; freeze. If desired, insert popsicle sticks when mixture is partially frozen.


# STRAWBERRY BREAD

**3 C. flour**    **1/2 tsp. salt**
**2 C. sugar**    **1 T. baking powder**
**1 tsp. vanilla**    **1 tsp. cinnamon**
**1/2 C. vegetable oil**    **4 eggs, beaten**
**2 C. sliced strawberries,**    **2/3 C. chopped nuts**
   **sweetened with 1/2 C. sugar**

Blend all ingredients thoroughly. Pour into 2 greased and floured loaf pans. Bake at 350 degrees for 40 minutes.


# EASY RASPBERRY FROST

**1-3 oz. pkg. raspberry gelatin**    **1-11 oz. can mandarin**
**1 C. boiling water**      **oranges, drained**
**1 pint raspberry sherbert**    **2 C. miniature marshmallows**

Add boiling water to gelatin; stir well to completely dissolve. Add sherbert, stir until dissolved. Chill until slightly thickened. Fold in fruit and marshmallows. Chill until firm.

# PINEAPPLE WHIP

**1-20 oz. can crushed pineapple,**
   **drained**
**1-14 oz. can sweetened,**
   **milk condensed**

**1/4 C. lemon juice**
**1/2 C. chopped nuts**
**1-12 oz. frozen whipped**
   **topping, thawed**

Mix pineapple, lemon juice, and sweetened condensed milk in a bowl. Fold in whipped topping and nuts.  Chill for 5 to 6 hours.

# NOTES:

_____

_____

_____

_____

_____

_____

_____

_____

_____

_____

_____

_____

_____

_____

_____

_____

_____

_____

_____

_____

# MISCELLANEOUS

# My Favorites

## COFFEE-CAKE MUFFINS

1 1/2 c. flour
2 tsp. baking powder
1/4 tsp. baking soda
1/4 tsp. salt
1/4 C. shortening
8 oz. sour cream
1/2 C. granulated sugar

1/2 C. milk
1 egg, beaten
1/4 C. packed brown sugar
1/4 C. chopped nuts
2 T. granulated sugar
1 tsp. cinnamon

In a large bowl, stir together the flour, baking powder, baking soda, and salt. Cut in the shortening until the flour mixture is crumbly. In another bowl, stir together the sour cream, the 1/2 C. granulated (Complete Receipe on page 110)

## HOT DOG SAUCE

Page 111

1 lb. ground beef
1 1/2 tsp. paprika
Water

1 1/2 tsp. chili powder, or to taste
1 tsp. cumin powder

Brown ground beef, stirring often to create a fine texture; drain well. Add just enough water to cover beef. Add paprika, chili powder, and cumin. Simmer 35 to 45 minutes. If mixture is too thin, thicken with 1 T. flour.
(Complete Recipe on page 111)

# GRILLED RANCH BREAD

**1/2 C. softened butter**
**1 loaf French or Italian bread**

**1-1 oz. pkg. Ranch dressing mix**

Slices loaf of bread lengthwise. Combine softened butter and Ranch dressing mix. Spread mixture on bread. Place on grill, buttered side down and grill until crispy and golden brown.


# PICKLED EGGS

**1 doz. eggs**
**2-15 oz. cans beet chunks**

**1/3 C. sugar**
**2/3 C. vinegar**

Hard boil eggs and peel. In a bowl, mix vinegar and sugar together. Put 1 can of beets including liquid and 6 eggs into a 2-qt. glass jar. Pour in the vinegar and sugar mixture. Put lid on jar and gently shake until well blended. Put remaining 1 can of beets and 6 eggs into the jar and fill jar with water to within 1" of top. Put lid on and gently shake as before. Let sit in the refrigerator for 2 to 3 days.

TIP: Beet juice stains easily, so put a towel over the lid of the jar when shaking and shake over the sink in case of spills. Once eggs are gone, juice can be used a second time for another batch.


# SOUR CREAM CUCUMBERS

**2 to 3 large cucumbers, sliced**
**1-16 oz. sour cream**
**Sprinkle of salt and pepper**

**1/4 C. vinegar**
**1/4 C. sugar**

Stir sour cream until smooth. Slowly add vinegar, stirring until smooth. Add sugar, salt and pepper; stir. Pour mixture over cucumbers and gently mix to coat.

For thinner sauce, increase vinegar and sugar to 1/2 cup.

# COFFEE-CAKE MUFFINS

1 1/2 c. flour
2 tsp. baking powder
1/4 tsp. baking soda
1/4 tsp. salt
1/4 C. shortening
8 oz. sour cream
1/2 C. granulated sugar
1/2 C. milk
1 egg, beaten
1/4 C. packed brown sugar
1/4 C. chopped nuts
2 T. granulated sugar
1 tsp. cinnamon

In a large bowl, stir together the flour, baking powder, baking soda, and salt. Cut in the shortening until the flour mixture is crumbly. In another bowl, stir together the sour cream, the 1/2 C. granulated sugar, milk, and egg. Add the sour cream mixture to the dry ingredients and stir just until combined. In another bowl, combine the brown sugar, nuts, the 2 T. granulated sugar, and cinnamon. Line muffin tins with paper baking cups. Spoon half the batter into muffin cups. Sprinkle half the nut mixture into the cups. Top with remaining batter and remaining nut mixture. Bake at 350 degrees for 15 to 20 minutes or until a toothpick inserted in center comes out clean. Cool 5 minutes.

Can be served with a cup of coffee for breakfast or with ice cream as a dessert. Best if served warm.


# HOMEMADE PLAY DOUGH

1 C. flour
1/2 C. salt
2 tsp. cream of tartar
1 C. water
1 tsp. vegetable oil
Food coloring

Combine flour, salt, and cream of tartar. Add water, oil, and food coloring; stir. In a heavy skillet, cook the mixture for 2 to 3 minutes, stirring frequently. Knead dough until soft and smooth. Store in containers—butter tubs work well.

TIP: Make batches of several colors and let the kids have fun!!

# TOMATO JUICE COCKTAIL

1-14 oz. can tomato juice     1/4 tsp. Worcestershire sauce
1/2 tsp. onion, grated     1/2 tsp. sugar
1 tsp. celery, chopped     1/2 tsp. salt
2 T. lemon juice     1/2 tsp. horseradish

Combine all ingredients and chill I hour.  Strain and serve.

Add a shot of vodka and a stalk of celery for a great Bloody Mary!


# FRUIT PUNCH COCKTAIL

1/2 shot Peach Schnapps     1/2 shot cranberry juice
1/2 shot coconut rum     Orange juice
1 shot vodka

Pour all ingredients into a large glass of ice, ending with enough orange juice to fill the glass.  Enjoy!


# HOT DOG SAUCE

1 lb. ground beef     1 1/2 tsp. chili powder,
1 1/2 tsp. paprika       or to taste
Water     1 tsp. cumin powder

Brown ground beef, stirring often to create a fine texture; drain well. Add just enough water to cover beef.  Add paprika, chili powder, and cumin.  Simmer 35 to 45 minutes.  If mixture is too thin, thicken with 1 T. flour.

This hot dog sauce freezes well.

## SWEET AND SOUR SAUCE

3/4 C. apricot preserves
1/2 C. real mayonnaise
1/2 C. ketchup

1/4 C. soy sauce
1 tsp. ginger

Whisk all ingredients together until smooth. Brush on meats, turning frequently, during last 20 minutes of cooking.

## STUFFED PIG STOMACH

1 pig stomach
Sausage
Potatoes
Salt

Pepper
Onion
Cabbage

Clean pig stomach well by taking out the inside lining. Dice the potatoes, and onion. Shred the cabbage. Combine the sausage, potatoes, onion, and cabbage. Season with salt and pepper. Put mixture into the stomach; sew opening up. Put in a roaster and add about 2" of water. Grill for about 3 hours, adding water as necessary, or until meat and vegetables are done.

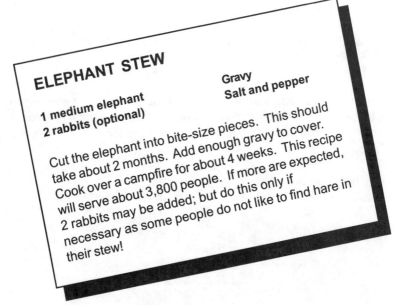

ELEPHANT STEW

1 medium elephant
2 rabbits (optional)

Gravy
Salt and pepper

Cut the elephant into bite-size pieces. This should take about 2 months. Add enough gravy to cover. Cook over a campfire for about 4 weeks. This recipe will serve about 3,800 people. If more are expected, 2 rabbits may be added; but do this only if necessary as some people do not like to find hare in their stew!

## GRAMMA'S RECIPE FOR A HAPPY DAY

Take a little dash of cold water, a little leaven of prayer, a little bit of sunshine; dissolve in morning air. Add to your meal more merriment; add thought for kith and kin; and then, as a prime ingredient, plenty of work thrown in. Flavor it with essence of love; add a dash of play. Let the Dear Old Book and a glance above, complete the well spent day.

In memory of the author's Great-Gramma Heifner.

# NOTES:

_____

_____

_____

_____

_____

_____

_____

_____

_____

_____

_____

_____

_____

_____

_____

_____

_____

_____

_____

_____

_____

_____

# "HOUSEHOLD HINTS"

Tips to remedy this or
that in the household

# TABLE OF CONTENTS

## COMMON KITCHEN PANS TO USE

**WHEN THE RECIPE CALLS FOR:**
**4-cup baking dish:**
9-inch pie plate                                                    A
8 x 1 1/4-inch layer cake pan - C
7 3/8 x 3 5/8 x 2 1/4-inch loaf pan - A
**6-cup baking dish:**                                              B
8 or 9 x 1 1/2-inch layer-cake pan - C
10-inch pie plate
8 1/2 x 3 5/8 x 2 5/8-inch loaf pan - A                             C
**8-cup baking dish:**
8 x 8 x 2-inch square pan - D
11 x 7 x 1 1/2-inch baking pan                                      D
9 x 5 x 3-inch loaf pan - A
**10-cup baking dish:**
9 x 9 x 2-inch square pan                                           E
11 3/4 x 7 1/2 x 1 3/4-inch baking pan - D
15 x 10 x 1-inch jellyroll pan
**12-cup baking dish or over:**                                     F
12 1/3 x 8 1/2 x 2-inch glass baking pan -        12 cups
13 x 9 x 2-inch metal baking pan -                15 cups
14 x 10 1/2 x 2 1/2-inch roasting -               19 cups  G

**TOTAL VOLUME OF VARIOUS SPECIAL BAKING PANS**
**Tube Pans:**
7 1/2 x 3-inch "Bundt" tube - K -                 6 cups    H
9 x 3 1/2-inch fancy tube or "Bundt" pan-J or K-  9 cups
9 x 3 1/2-inch angel cake pan - H -               12 cups
10 x 3 3/4-inch "Bundt" or "Crownburst" pan-K-    12 cups  J
9 x 3 1/2-inch fancy tube - J -                    12 cups
10 x 4-inch fancy tube mold (kugelhupf)-J-        16 cups
10 x 4-inch angel cake pan - H -                  18 cups
**Spring-Form Pans:**
8 x 3-inch pan - B -                              12 cups   K
9 x 3-inch pan - B -                              16 cups
**Ring Mold:**
8 1/2 x 2 1/4-inch mold - E -                     4 1/2 cups
9 1/4 x 2 3/4-inch mold - E -                     8 cups
**Charlotte Mold:**
6 x 4 1/4-inch mold - G -                         7 1/2 cups
**Brioche Pan:**
9 1/2 x 3 1/4-inch pan -  F -                     8 cups

## QUANTITIES TO SERVE 100 PEOPLE

| | |
|---|---|
| Coffee | 3 lbs. |
| Cream | 3 qts. |
| Whipping cream | 4 pts. |
| Milk | 6 gallons |
| Fruit cocktail | 2 1/2 gallons |
| Fruit juice | 4 #10 cans |
| Tomato juice | 4 #10 cans |
| Soup | 5 gallons |
| Hot Dogs | 25 lbs. |
| Meat loaf | 18 to 22 lbs. |
| Ham | 40 lbs. |
| Beef | 40 lbs. |
| Roast pork | 40 lbs. |
| Hamburger | 30 to 36 lbs. |
| Chicken for chicken pie | 40 lbs. |
| Potatoes | 35 lbs. |
| Scalloped potatoes | 4 gals. |
| Spaghetti | 5 gals. |
| Vegetables | 4 #10 cans |
| Baked beans | 5 gals. |
| Beets | 25 lbs. |
| Cauliflower | 18 lbs. |
| Cabbage for slaw | 16 lbs. |
| Carrots | 24 lbs. |
| Corn | 2 #10 cans |
| Bread | 10 loaves |
| Rolls | 200 |
| Butter | 3 lbs. |
| Potato salad | 3 1/2 to 4 gals. |
| Fruit salad | 20 qts. |
| Vegetable salad | 20 qts. |
| Lettuce | 16 lg. heads |
| Salad dressing | 3 qts. |
| Jello | 2 1/2 qts. |
| Pies | 18 |
| Cakes | 8 |
| Ice Cream | 4 gallons |
| Cheese | 3 lbs. |
| Olives | 1 3/4 lbs. |
| Pickles | 2 qts. |
| Nuts | 3 lbs. |

To serve 50 people, divide by 2. To serve 25 people, divide by 4. Cooking for a crowd. The season of the year rules the food choices to a degree. Also variety in flavor, texture, color and form. Plan best use of refrigerator space. Decide type of service, buffet, family style or served plates with waitresses.

## CONTENTS OF CANS

*Of the different sizes of cans used by commercial canners, the most common are:*

| Size | Average Contents |
|---|---|
| 8 ounces | 1 cup |
| picnic | 1 1/4 cups |
| No. 300 | 1 3/4 cups |
| No. 1 tall | 2 cups |
| No. 303 | 2 cups |
| No. 2 | 2 1/2 cups |
| No. 2 1/2 | 3 1/2 cups |
| No. 3 | 4 cups |
| No. 10 | 12 to 13 cups |

## SUBSTITUTIONS

**FOR:**                                     **YOU CAN USE:**

1 T. cornstarch .......................... 2 T. flour OR 1 1/2 T. quick
cooking tapioca

1 C. cake flour .......................... 1 C. less 2 T. all-purpose flour

1 C. all-purpose flour ............... 1 C. plus 2 T. cake flour

1 square chocolate .................. 3 T. cocoa and 1 T. fat

1 C. melted shortening ............ 1 C. salad oil (may not be substituted
for solid shortening)

1 C. milk .................................. 1/2 C. evaporated milk and 1/2 C. water

1 C. sour milk or buttermilk ..... 1 T. lemon juice or vinegar and enough
sweet milk to measure 1 C.

1 C. heavy cream .................... 2/3 C. milk and 1/3 C. butter

1 C. heavy cream, whipped     2/3 C. well-chilled evaporated milk,
whipped

Sweetened condensed milk .... No substitution

1 egg ....................................... 2 T. dried whole egg and 2 T. water

1 tsp. baking powder ............... 1/4 tsp. baking soda and 1 tsp. cream
of tartar OR 1/4 tsp. baking soda and
1/2 C. sour milk, buttermilk or molasses;
reduce other liquid 1/2 C.

1 C. sugar................................ 1 C. honey; reduce other liquid 1/4 C.;
reduce baking temperature 25°

1 C. miniature marshmallows .. About 10 large marshmallows, cut up

1 medium onion (2 1/2" dia.) ... 2 T. instant minced onion OR 1 tsp.
onion powder OR 2 tsp. onion salt;
reduce salt 1 tsp.

1 garlic clove .......................... 1/8 tsp. garlic powder OR 1/4 tsp. garlic
salt reduce salt 1/8 tsp.

1 T. fresh herbs ...................... 1 tsp. dried herbs OR 1/4 tsp. powdered
herbs OR 1/2 tsp. herb salt; reduce salt
1/4 tsp.

## SUBSTITUTIONS

**For bread crumbs:** Use crushed corn or wheat flakes, or other dry cereal. Or use potato flakes.

**For butter:** Use 7/8 cup of solid shortening plus 1/2 teaspoon of salt.

**For fresh milk:** To substitute 1 cup of fresh milk, use 1/2 cup each of evaporated milk and water.

For 1 cup of whole milk, prepare 1 liquid cup of nonfat dry milk and 2 1/2 teaspoons butter or margarine.

**For sugar:** Use brown sugar, although it will result in a slight molasses flavor.

**For superfine sugar:** Process regular granulated sugar in your blender.

**For red and green sweet pepper:** Use canned pimientos.

**For vanilla extract:** Use grated lemon or orange rind for flavoring instead. Or try a little cinnamon or nutmeg.

**For flour:** Use 1 tablespoon cornstarch instead of 2 tablespoons of flour. Or try using instant potatoes or cornmeal.

**For buttermilk:** Use 1 tablespoon of lemon juice or vinegar and enough fresh milk to make 1 cup. Let it stand 5 minutes before using.

**For catsup:** Use a cup of tomato sauce added to 1 1/4 cups of brown sugar, 2 tablespoons of vinegar, 1/4 teaspoon of cinnamon and a dash of ground cloves and allspice.

**For unsweetened chocolate:** Use 1 tablespoon of shortening plus 3 tablespoons of unsweetened chocolate to equal 1 square of unsweetened chocolate.

**For corn syrup:** Use 1/4 cup of water or other type of liquid called for in the recipe, plus 1 cup of sugar.

**For eggs:** Add 3 or 4 extra tablespoons of liquid called for in the recipe. Or, when you're 1 egg shy for a recipe that calls for many, substitute 1 teaspoon of cornstarch.

**For cake flour:** Use 7/8 cup of all-purpose flour for each cup of cake flour called for in a recipe.

**For fresh herbs and spices:** For 1/3 the amount of dried herbs or spices. Dried herbs are more concentrated.

**For honey:** To substitute 1 cup of honey, use 1 1/4 cups of sugar and 1/4 cup of water or other liquid called for in the recipe.

## DEEP-FAT FRYING TEMPERATURES WITHOUT A THERMOMETER

**A 1-inch cube of white bread will turn golden brown:**

| | |
|---|---|
| 345° to 355° | 65 seconds |
| 355° to 365° | 60 seconds |
| 365° to 375° | 50 seconds |
| 375° to 385° | 40 seconds |
| 385° to 395° | 20 seconds |

## OVEN TEMPERATURES

| | |
|---|---|
| Slow | 300° |
| Slow moderate | 325° |
| Moderate | 350° |
| Quick moderate | 375° |
| Moderately hot | 400° |
| Hot | 425° |
| Very Hot | 475° |

## SIMPLIFIED MEASURES

| Measure | Equivalent |
| --- | --- |
| 1 tablespoon | 3 teaspoons |
| 2 tablespoons | 1 ounce |
| 1 jigger | 1 1/2 ounces |
| 1/4 cup | 4 tablespoons |
| 1/3 cup | 5 tablespoons plus 1 teaspoon |
| 1/2 cup | 8 tablespoons |
| 1 cup | 16 tablespoons |
| 1 pint | 2 cups |
| 1 quart | 4 cups |
| 1 gallon | 4 quarts |
| 1 liter | 4 cups plus 3 tablespoons |
| 1 ounce (dry) | 2 tablespoons |
| 1 pound | 16 ounces |
| 2.21 pounds | 35.3 ounces |

## FOOD GUIDE PYRAMID

A Guide to Daily Food Choices

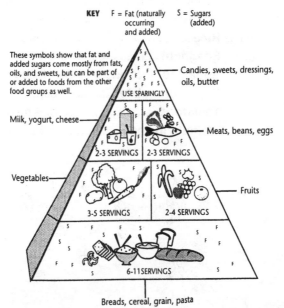

**KEY**    F = Fat (naturally occurring and added)    S = Sugars (added)

These symbols show that fat and added sugars come mostly from fats, oils, and sweets, but can be part of or added to foods from the other food groups as well.

USE SPARINGLY

Candies, sweets, dressings, oils, butter

Milk, yogurt, cheese — 2-3 SERVINGS

Meats, beans, eggs — 2-3 SERVINGS

Vegetables — 3-5 SERVINGS

Fruits — 2-4 SERVINGS

6-11 SERVINGS

Breads, cereal, grain, pasta

## EQUIVALENTS FOR COMMON COOKING INGREDIENTS

| | | |
|---|---|---|
| 1 lb. | **Apples** | 3 or 4 medium |
| 1 lb. | **Bananas** | 3 or 4 medium |
| 1 lb. | **Beans, dried** | 5 to 6 cups cooked |
| 1 quart | **Berries** | 3 1/2 cups |
| 1 slice | **Bread** | 1/2 cup crumbs |
| 1/4 lb. | **Cheese, grated** | 1 cup |
| 1 oz. | **Chocolate, 1 square** | 1 T. melted |
| 1/2 pint | **Cream** | 1 cup |
| 1 cup | **Cream, heavy** | 2 cups whipped |
| 1 lb. | **Flour, all-purpose** | 4 cups sifted |
| 1 envelope | **Gelatin** | 1 T. |
| 1 tsp. | **Herbs, dried** | 1 T. fresh |
| 2-3 T. juice | **Lemon** | 1 1/2 tsp. grated rind |
| 1 cup dry | **Macaroni** | 2 1/4 cups cooked |
| 1 lb. | **Meat, diced** | 2 cups |
| 1 lb. | **Mushrooms** | 5-6 cups sliced |
| 1/4 lb. | **Nuts, shelled** | 1 cup chopped |
| 1 medium | **Onion** | 1/2 cup chopped |
| 6-8 T. juice | **Orange** | 1/3-1/2 cup pulp |
| 3 medium | **Potatoes** | 1 3/4 - 2 cups mashed |
| 1 cup uncooked | **Rice** | 3 cups cooked |
| 1/2 lb. | **Spaghetti** | 3 1/2 - 4 cups cooked |
| 1 lb. | **Sugar, confectioners** | 4 1/2 cups unsifted |
| 1 lb. | **Sugar, granulated** | 2 cups |
| 1 lb. | **Tomatoes** | 3 or 4 medium |
| 1 lb. | **Walnuts in shell** | 1 3/4 cups chopped |

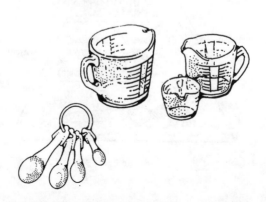

## COMMON CAUSES OF FAILURE IN BAKING

### BISCUITS
1. Rough biscuits caused from insufficient mixing.
2. Dry biscuits caused from baking in too slow an oven and handling too much.
3. Uneven browning caused from cooking in dark surface pan (use a cookie sheet or shallow bright finish pan), too high a temperature and rolling the dough too thin.

### MUFFINS
1. Coarse texture caused from insufficient stirring and cooking at too low a temperature.
2. Tunnels in muffins, peaks in center and soggy texture are caused from overmixing.
3. For a nice muffin, mix well but light and bake at correct temperature.

### CAKES
1. Cracks and uneven surface may be caused by too much flour, too hot an oven and sometimes from cold oven start.
2. Cake is dry may be caused by too much flour, too little shortening, too much baking powder or cooking at too low a temperature.
3. A heavy cake means too much sugar has been used or baked too short a period.
4. A sticky crust is caused by too much sugar.
5. Coarse grained cake may be caused by too little mixing, too much fat, too much baking powder, using fat too soft, and baking at too low a temperature.
6. Cakes fall may be caused by using insufficient flour, under baking, too much sugar, too much fat or not enough baking powder.
7. Uneven browning may be caused from cooking cakes at too high a temperature, crowding the shelf (allow at least 2" around pans) or using dark pans (use bright finish, smooth bottomed pans).
8. Cake has uneven color is caused from not mixing well. Mix thoroughly, but do not over mix.

### PIES
1. Pastry crumbles caused by overmixing flour and fat.
2. Pastry is tough caused by using too much water and over mixing dough.
3. Pies do not burn - for fruit or custard pies use a Pyrex pie pan or enamel pan and bake at 400° to 425° constant temperature.

### BREADS (YEAST)
1. Yeast bread is porous - this is caused by over-rising or cooking at too low a temperature.
2. Crust is dark and blisters - this is caused by over-rising, the bread will blister just under the crust.
3. Bread does not rise - this is caused from over-kneading or from using old yeast.
4. Bread is streaked - this is caused from underkneading and not kneading evenly.
5. Bread baked uneven - caused by using old dark pans, too much dough in pan, crowding the oven shelf or cooking at too high temperature.

## WHAT TO USE SPICES AND SEASONINGS FOR!

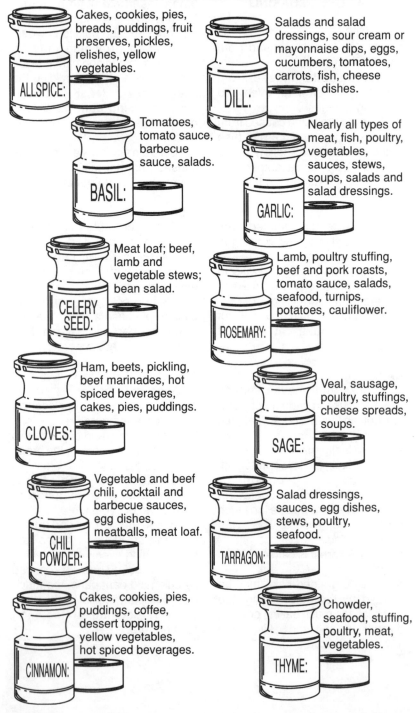

**ALLSPICE:** Cakes, cookies, pies, breads, puddings, fruit preserves, pickles, relishes, yellow vegetables.

**DILL:** Salads and salad dressings, sour cream or mayonnaise dips, eggs, cucumbers, tomatoes, carrots, fish, cheese dishes.

**BASIL:** Tomatoes, tomato sauce, barbecue sauce, salads.

**GARLIC:** Nearly all types of meat, fish, poultry, vegetables, sauces, stews, soups, salads and salad dressings.

**CELERY SEED:** Meat loaf; beef, lamb and vegetable stews; bean salad.

**ROSEMARY:** Lamb, poultry stuffing, beef and pork roasts, tomato sauce, salads, seafood, turnips, potatoes, cauliflower.

**CLOVES:** Ham, beets, pickling, beef marinades, hot spiced beverages, cakes, pies, puddings.

**SAGE:** Veal, sausage, poultry, stuffings, cheese spreads, soups.

**CHILI POWDER:** Vegetable and beef chili, cocktail and barbecue sauces, egg dishes, meatballs, meat loaf.

**TARRAGON:** Salad dressings, sauces, egg dishes, stews, poultry, seafood.

**CINNAMON:** Cakes, cookies, pies, puddings, coffee, dessert topping, yellow vegetables, hot spiced beverages.

**THYME:** Chowder, seafood, stuffing, poultry, meat, vegetables.

## WHICH APPLES ARE BEST?

**BAKING:** Albermarle Pippin, Granny Smith, Jonathan, Rome Beauty
**EATING:** Red and Yellow Delicious, Grimes Golden, Rome Beauty
**PIE:** Granny Smith, Grimes Golden, Rome Beauty, Stayman, Winesap
**SALAD:** Granny Smith, Grimes Golden, Red Delicious, Rome Beauty, York Imperial, Winesap
**SAUCE:** Early Harvest, Summer Rambo, Grimes Golden, Stayman, Winesap, York Imperial

## APPLES

• Place apple cider in 32 cup p e r c o l a t o r coffeemaker and fill c o f f e e  basket 1/2 full of red-hot candies. Makes tasty spicy pink cider.
• Premeasure and freeze apple slices for Apple Crisp recipes.
• Substitute apples for blueberries in muffins.
• Put 2 tablespoons apple juice concentrate in cream cheese frosting for applesauce cupcakes.
• Keep apples from absorbing strong refrigerator odors by storing them in a plastic bag. They will stay fresher longer and won't speed ripening of other produce.
• Toss lemon juice on cut-up apples to prevent browning.
• Add 1/2 cup extra apples to a pie that you wish "very full".
• Cut apple in half horizontally. Cut design in apple halves and use for stamps to decorate. Kids love this!

## BARBECUES

• It's simple to grill acorn s q u a s h . Pierce the skin with fork a couple of times, then wrap in aluminum foil. Grill over direct heat for 1 hour turning once. Remove from grill.
• Store already made hamburger patties on tray between waxed paper. Can lift for accessibility once grilling starts.
• For tender flavorful spareribs begin by parboiling them in pineapple juice. Then add a homemade barbecue sauce while grilling.
• Leftover barbecued pork chops make great sandwiches. Just remove meat from bones, reheat and serve on buns.
• Here's an easy marinade for grilled pork chops; for four chops, combine 1/2 cup each soy sauce, water and honey. Pour over chops and marinate, leave covered in the refrigerator overnight. Grill until done as desired.
• For fast, easy cleanup of food stuck inside pans, boil a little vinegar and water in the pan before washing. No scrubbing is required–the pan practically wipes clean.
• Instead of taking time to make meatballs make "meat squares". Spread meat mixture in jelly roll pan and bake over coals or in oven. Cut in small squares.
• To roast corn, pull back husks and remove silks. Replace husks and tie at top. Soak in salt water for 1 hour. Grill over hot coals for 15 to 20 minutes turning frequently.
• Old baking pans (even garage sale finds) clean up easily after grilling if they are completely covered with aluminum foil first. Once the cooking is done just remove foil and discard.

• Presoak bamboo skewers in water for 20 minutes before threading with meat, veggies or fruit to prevent them from scorching or burning.
• Venison or turkey burgers will not stick to grill when they are coated with nonstick cooking spray.

## BERRIES

• Using a potato blender is quicker than using a fork for m a s h i n g strawberries.
• Berries will keep up to a week refrigerated unwashed and unsweetened in a loosely covered container.
• When picking strawberries look under the leaves for the best berries as they will hide there.
• Thawed frozen berries will always be softer and juicier than fresh berries. Defrost the sealed bag of frozen berries in a larger bowl of cold water for 10 to 15 minutes, then use them in recipes where the extra juice is a bonus, such as over shortcake or in a sauce for pound cake.
• Strawberries can be used in punches as a garnish, in the ice ring itself, or as the base for a delicious punch. The berries can be mashed, strained to eliminate the seeds and doctored up as per recipe or imagination.
• Premeasure berries, rhubarb, etc. for future baking projects in amounts called for in favorite recipes. Prevents messy measuring later.
• Best way to pick berries is to pinch and twist the stems, leaving the hulls intact.
• Remove stem and hull from fresh strawberries with a tomato corer.
• Use sliced or mashed strawberries sprinkled with sugar for shortcake.

If they stand for 20 to 30 minutes they will make their juice.
• Use whole strawberries with pointed ends facing upward if you plan to glaze recipe.
• Use egg slicer for cutting perfect slices of strawberries.
• Strawberries are best if picked red and firm, but may be ripened if left on counter for a day.
• For shortcake or scones use a rich hot fudge strawberry filling with one cup warmed hot topping and one cup sliced strawberries.

## BREADS

• Always b r u s h the tops of your yeast breads and rolls with melted butter when you put the dough into the pans, but do it before it raises a final time. Use just enough butter to glaze the top. This adds flavor and brown color. Brush tops again with soft butter.
• Add butterscotch chips to batter of pumpkin quick bread instead of raisins. More delicious!
• Shredded green tomatoes may be substituted for zucchini in a zucchini bread recipe.
• Homemade bread contains no preservatives and needs refrigeration.
• Bread that sounds hollow when tapped with fingers is baked perfectly.
• Dough rises better if kept out of drafts. Cover with towel and set over a pilot light on stove (if you have one). Let dough "rest" before rolling it out to shape it–it will be less elastic and easier to handle.
• Knead dough in a large resealable bag. Hands and countertops stay clean.

• Turn your basic recipe for 2 or 3 loaves of whole wheat bread into one for herb bread by adding 1/4 teaspoon each of marjoram, thyme, oregano and garlic powder and 1 tablespoon grated onion. Mix into the warm water or milk before adding the flour.

• For a crisp crust, brush the unbaked loaf with lightly beaten egg white. For a soft crust, brush the baked loaf with melted butter when it comes out of oven.

• Remove bread from pan to cool, so bottom will not stay moist.

• Bake quick breads one day before serving. Wrap and refrigerate. They have better texture and will slice better also.

• Don't overmix your batter when making quick bread or muffins. The finished product may crumble. Muffin batter should be lumpy.

• Brush Christmas yeast coffee cakes with lightly beaten egg white before baking. Then sprinkle with slivered almonds and white or colored sugar.

• When dissolving yeast, always remember to put about 1 teaspoon of sugar into lukewarm water or milk. It helps to get the dough working so yeast will raise. If yeast doesn't work you'll have a clump.

• For quick and easy garlic bread-sticks; split a hot dog bun down the middle and cut each 1/2 lengthwise. Butter each strip and sprinkle with garlic salt or powder. Place on baking sheet and broil until toasted.

• Put frozen bread loaves in a clean brown paper bag and place for 5 minutes in a 325° oven to thaw completely.

## BREAKFAST

• Keep bacon slices from sticking together; heat a spatula over a burner, slide it under each slice to separate it from others.

• Use egg slicer to slice Kiwi uniformly.

• For a perfect fried egg, put a little butter, bacon grease, or side pork fat into a skillet (cast iron is best). If you want it sunny-side up, put a cover on and the steam will take care of the egg. if you want it over easy, flip the egg over, and count to five slowly. Leave it longer if you like the yolks hard.

• For crispy French toast, add a touch of cornstarch to the egg mixture.

• To butter many slices of bread quickly and evenly, heat the butter until soft. Then use a pastry brush to paint the butter on.

• For fluffier omelettes, add a pinch of cornstarch before beating.

• To ripen Kiwi's, place them in a brown paper bag with a banana or apple and leave at room temperature. When they are ready to eat, they should yield to slight pressure. Store ripe fruit in refrigerator for up to one week.

• To make an inexpensive syrup for pancakes, save small amounts of leftover jams and jellies in a jar. Or, fruit-flavored syrup can be made by adding 2 cups sugar to 1 cup of any kind of fruit juice and cooking until it boils.

• Freeze waffles that are left; they can be reheated in the toaster.

## CAKES AND FROSTINGS

• When testing cake for doneness the rack may be pulled out a little only as it needs to stay close to the heat. Test with either toothpick or touch lightly with fingertips. If the cake bounces back it is done, if it leaves a dent, then it's not.

• To keep a cake from sliding on its plate during transit, drizzle a bit of frosting in a circle on the plate where the cake will rest before removing the cake from the pan. The frosting will hold the cake in place.

• Don't tamper with the mix or change it. If it says cream it means cream. If it says 2% then it means 2%.

• Sweeten whipped cream with confectioners' sugar instead of granulated sugar. It will stay fluffy and hold up a lot longer.

• Always refrigerate cream cheese-based frostings and fillings.

• Always let a cake cool 10 minutes before running a knife around the edge and turning out on a plate. An upside-down cake or jelly roll has to be removed at once.

• Spray measuring spoons or cups with a coating of nonstick cooking spray before measuring honey, syrup, or molasses. Sticky ingredients slide right out with no mess.

• If it calls for sour milk, and you have none, put 1 tablespoon of vinegar in one cup of milk, it will curdle immediately.

• Be sure your rack is in the center of the oven or the cake will come out too brown either on the top or bottom.

• If you are getting lopsided cakes then level up your stove.

• To prevent icing from running off your cake, try dusting the surface lightly with cornstarch before icing.

• If you forget to preheat the oven, turn the broiler on for a minute to get the temperature up fast.

• To dress up a plain frosted cake but have no sprinkles—crush sweetened cereal and scatter across the top. Adds a fun look and a nice crunch, too.

• When it says to grease pan, it means only the bottom as the cake has to have something to hold on to.

• To prepare muffins or cupcakes easily mix the batter in a pitcher so it can be poured in cups without making a mess.

• To improve an inexpensive cake mix, add one tablespoon of butter to the batter. This will make a richer-tasting cake.

• Try a little cream of tartar in your 7 minute icing, it will not get dry and cracked.

• Shortly before taking cupcakes from the oven, place a marshmallow on each for quick frosting.

• In place of flour use one teaspoon of tapioca for thickening in fruit pies.

## COOKIES

• Flour the rolling pin slightly and roll lightly to desired thickness. Cut shapes close together and keep all trimmings for the last. Place pans in upper 1/3 of oven. Watch cookies carefully while baking to avoid burning edges.

• Beat butter and sugar at medium speed. Beat dry ingredients at low speed. Don't overbeat. The dough should be just blended.

• Use only stick butter or margarine in these recipes. Don't use reduced-fat or tub products. The fat and moisture content will yield poor results.

• For best results, bake one sheet of cookies at a time on the center rack of your oven. You can bake two sheets—halfway through baking, switch the pans from one rack to the other.

• Use outline (not solid) cookie cutters for napkins rings when having a party or country setting.

• Use electric knife to slice rolled-chilled cookie dough.

• For accuracy, measure liquids in clear measuring cups with spouts and hold the cup to eye level.

• Add 1/2 cup of sour cream to your peanut butter cookie recipe to make your cookies more moist.

• Most cookies can be stored at room temperature for a few days without losing flavor. For longer storage, place cookies and wax paper in layers in airtight container and freeze for 3 months.

• For chewy cookies, bake until edges are golden and the center looks slightly underbaked. Cool on baking sheets for 1 to 2 minutes before removing to a wire rack.

• When sprinkling sugar on cookies, try putting it into a salt shaker, as it saves time.

• Use nesting metal cups and spoons to measure flour and other dry ingredients. Before measuring, stir flour in its canister or package to aerate, then spoon it into appropriate-size measuring cup. Level off any excess with a metal spatula.

• Cookie dough that is to be rolled is much easier to handle after it has been in a cold place for 10 to 30 minutes. This keeps it from sticking, even though it may be soft. If not done, the dough may require more flour and too much flour makes the cookies hard and brittle. In rolling, take out on a floured board only as much dough as can be managed easily.

Lay a dampened cloth on your table or countertop before putting the cookie sheet down so it won't slide around while you fill it.

• Stale angel food cake can be cut into 1/2" slices and shaped with cookie cutters to make delicious "cookies". Just toast in the oven for a few minutes.

## EGGS

• If you shake the egg and you hear a rattle, you can be sure it's stale. A really fresh egg will sink and a stale one will float.

• If you are making deviled eggs and want to slice it perfectly, dip the knife in water first. The slice will be smooth with no yolk sticking to the knife.

• The white of an egg is easiest to beat when it's at room temperature. So leave it out of the refrigerator about a half an hour before using it.

• To make light and fluffy scrambled eggs, add a little water while beating the eggs.

• Add vinegar to the water while boiling eggs. Vinegar helps to seal the egg, since it acts on the calcium in the shell.

• Egg whites can be kept up to 1 year. Add them to a plastic container as you "collect them" for use in meringues, angel food cake...1 cup equals 7 or 8 egg whites. You can also refreeze defrosted egg whites.

• For fluffier omelets, add a pinch of cornstarch before beating.

• STORING EGGS: 1. Place your eggs in those tight-sealing egg containers and they will last longer in the refrigerator. You really shouldn't keep eggs longer than 11 days 2. Cover them with oil on the top in a sealed container in the refrigerator. 3. For long term storage: if there's a special on eggs at your local supermarket, you can take advantage of it. Just crack all the eggs open and put them in the freezer unit. To use one egg at a time, put single eggs in the ice tray. When frozen, put the egg cubes in a sealed plastic bag. You can take out the cubes one at a time for daily use. If you use eggs in twos or threes, freeze them that way in a plastic bag.

• To make quick-diced eggs, take your potato masher and go to work on a boiled egg.

• If you wrap each egg in aluminum foil before boiling it, the shell won't crack when it's boiling.

• To make those eggs go further when making scrambled eggs for a crowd, add a pinch of baking powder and 2 teaspoons of water per egg.

• A great trick for peeling eggs the easy way. When they are finished boiling, turn off the heat and just let them sit in the pan with the lid on for about 5 minutes. Steam will build up under the shell and they will just fall away.

• Or, quickly rinse hot hard-boiled eggs in cold water, and the shells will be easier to remove.

• Fresh or hard-boiled? Spin the egg. If it wobbles, it is raw - if it spins easily, it's hard boiled.

• Add a few drops of vinegar to the water when poaching an egg to keep it from running all over the pan.

• Add 1 tablespoon of water per egg white to increase the quantity of beaten egg white when making meringue.

• Fresh eggs are rough and chalky in appearance. Old eggs are smooth and shiny.

• Beaten egg whites will be more stable if you add 1 teaspoon cream of tartar to each cup of egg whites (7 or 8 eggs).

• Pierce the end of an egg with a pin, and it will not break when placed in boiling water.

• A small funnel is handy for separating egg whites from yolks. Open the egg over the funnel and the white will run through and the yolk will remain.

• For baking, it's best to use medium to large eggs. Extra large may cause cakes to fall when cooled.

• Brown and white shells are the same quantity.

## NUTS

• Use English walnuts and Black Walnut extract as a substitute for Black Walnuts.

• Cut nut bars into festive shapes for fun and variety at Holiday time.

• Freeze nuts in shells a few days before cracking. The nutmeats will come out in larger pieces if they are frozen.

• Make holiday treat of 1 1/2 lbs. white, dark or milk chocolate and one can of mixed nuts. Drop teaspoonfuls onto waxed paper to harden. Store in airtight container.

• Before chopping nuts in a food processor, dust them with flour. This keeps the nuts from sticking to the processor.

• Toasted almonds will chop easier than untoasted ones.

• To quickly crack a large amount of nuts, put in a bag and gently hammer until they are cracked open. Then remove nutmeats with a pick.

• Shake chopped nuts in flour before adding to cake batter. This prevents them from sinking to the bottom.

• Wear rubber gloves when husking Black Walnuts to prevent stains to the hands.

• Use a blender for quick coarsely chopped almonds.

• Pecans stay fresh in refrigerator for 9 months and in freezer for 2 years.

• If nuts are stale, place them in the oven at 250°F and leave them there for 5 or 10 minutes. The heat will revive them.

## PICKLING AND PRESERVING

• Quart jars are usually used for canning fruits, vegetables, meats and pickles. Pint jars are used for jams, preserves, relishes and sauces. Half-pint or jelly glasses are used for jams, jellies, butters and marmalades. The size of the family is important when choosing jar size.

• Pressure canning means to be done in a pressure cooker. Leave an inch space between jars after they have been taken out of the boiling water for air to circulate between the jars.

• Pickles and relishes can be eaten right away, but do get a better flavor the longer you wait. Dill pickles must wait 2 weeks.

• Use heavy stainless steel kettles when possible. Never cook vinegar in cheap aluminum as it will take on the taste.

• The number of jars you will get out of a recipe will vary because of the difference in the size and the moisture in the fruits and vegetables.

• For all canned pickles, relishes, and vegetables do not use iodized salt or the ingredients will get mushy.

• When filling jars always clean the tops off from spills.

• Syrups for jams and jellies will rise to top quickly and have to be watched very carefully.

• Spices may be added to pickles or relishes as are or may be tied up in a clean cloth, cooked with the pickles and discarded when cooking is done before jars are filled.

• Never sit hot jars in a draft.

• When they are cooling you will hear a popping if you are using the two-piece lids. That popping means that the jar has sealed. Press your finger on top; and if the cover is flat, it's okay. If jar has not sealed, use the contents–do not store.

• To scald your jars means to sterilize your empty jars by standing them upright in boiling water and filling with more boiling water and boil a minute or two.

• Sure-Jell helps set and speed-up jams and jellies but they can be cooked down low without it. Always ladle foam off of jams and jellies with a metal spoon.

## PIES

• Insert a knife into the slits of a double-crusted pie, and it should come out clear. If it is sugary it needs more baking.

• Spread meringue so it extends out to the edge of the crust so it won't pull away. It's sealed.

• Add 1 or 2 tablespoons of molasses to pumpkin pie filling. It will make it richer in color and tastier, too.

• Make nice fat pies and heap the filling into the crusts.

• Try not to make meringue on a humid day, since the sugar absorbs moisture and excess moisture may cause beading. Also be certain the sugar is completely dissolved during beating. Rub a small amount between your fingers-if it's grainy, continue to beat. Place the meringue over the hot filling. Keep filling warm while preparing meringue, pour it into the pie shell just before topping with meringue. Bake immediately at 350° for 15 minutes.

• Use a thimble to cut holes in your top pie crusts. Then replace cut-out circles back in their holes. The hole will get bigger as pie bakes, giving an interesting pattern.

• If recipe calls for milk, use whole milk. Store-bought does not have as much butterfat as farm milk, but it is just fine.

• No matter how much salt a recipe calls for—put it in there as it is there for a reason.

• Place your pastry-lined pie plate on a partially pulled-out oven rack, then carefully fill with mixture. Gently push rack in stove.

• Place a piece of plastic wrap over cooked custard or pudding after pouring into pie shell to prevent a "skin" from forming.

• Add one tablespoon sesame seeds to pie crust recipe to have a tasty nutty flavor.

• Be sure your rolling pin is wood and heavy enough. Some are too light. A medium pin weighs about 5 lbs. and is fine.

• If a recipe calls for a cup, don't put in a rounded cup. Unless it says "heaping", use only a level measure.

• When measuring shortening for pie crust wet the cup first, and the shortening will slide right out.

• Where a recipe calls for 2 cups freshly whipped cream, use 12 ounces of Cool Whip.

## SALADS

• Green peppers will not last long in the refrigerator. The best way to have them available is to freeze them. Wash them after hollowing out the insides, dry them and put them in a plastic bag. You can dice, strip, cube, or chip them.

• Iceberg lettuce as well as escarole and spinach is used for a bed for small and large salads, of any kind.

• The classic salad of iceberg lettuce is always welcome to the American table. It is used along with dressings or mixed with a variety of dark greens. It can be eaten dressed up very little or dressed up a lot with a variety of fruits, vegetables, meats, etc.

• Salads are light or complex and are usually chosen according to the meal they are served with. Fresh, tart greens will balance a heavy meal. A complex salad containing many ingredients will complement a lighter meal.

• Potato salads, a Waldorf salad, bean and mayo-dressed salads are generally informal, good picnic fare and healthy.

• Buffet salads are spreads with eye-appeal. They are molds, filled vegetable containers, marinated vegetables, and decoratively garnished salad platters.

• A basic earthy salad is nothing more than the edible parts of herbs and plants, gently seasoned with the most basic of spices or a sprinkling of lemon juice or vinegar and oil.

• Optimal freshness is the hallmark of a successful salad.

• Most salads should be served at room temperature.

• Commercial or homemade

dressings are a matter of choice.
• Flowers such as roses, daylillies, nasturtiums, geraniums and marigolds are commonly used in salads. They bruise easily so must be gotten early in the morning and handled carefully.
• Kale, beet greens, Swiss chard, bok choy, and the cabbages–including red, green and napa, and savory are all great additions to any salad, adding flavor and texture.
• To keep mint, lemon verbena, etc. from taking over your herb garden, pull your needed amounts by the roots. Enough root will remain for the plants to continue growing.
• Just about any cut of meat, fowl, or fish can be worked into a salad. Such salads can often be served as the main course. Remove all fat and gristle when preparing meat. Cut meat across the grain into even thickness strips. Arrange slices in a neat, decorative pattern on a platter.
• Place unripened tomatoes with other fruit, especially pears to speed up ripening.

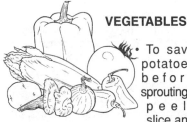

## VEGETABLES

• To save potatoes before sprouting– peel, slice and boil them partially. Drain, cool and freeze. When needed pop frozen potatoes into boiling water, finish cooking and then mash.
• Use an egg slicer to slice mushrooms perfectly.
• Use an ice cream scoop to remove seeds from acorn or Hubbard squash or even pumpkin seeds from pumpkins.
• Freeze your onion surplus. Slice or dice and bake in a covered casserole at 350° until they're tender, about 20 to 30 minutes. Cool and pack them in freezer containers in recipe-sized portions. Freeze for up to 6 months. To use, thaw and warm with a little butter until light golden brown–perfect for casseroles, burgers or in gravies.
• When cutting corn from the cob to freeze, place end of cob in the hole of a Bundt pan. Cut corn off with sharp knife and corn will fall right in pan with little mess.
• One pound of fresh spinach will yield 10 to 12 cups of torn leaves; which will cook down to about one cup.
• Put foil under sweet potatoes before baking so sticky juices can't mess up oven.
• Bake a potato casserole right along with your roast.
• Use nylon stocking to dry onions. Put one in toe, tie a knot, put in onion, tie a knot-continue to stocking top. Hang in dry place. When needed cut one off between knots.
• Cook equal amounts of potatoes and turnips in boiling salted water until tender. Mash with milk and butter. Real treat!
• To preserve garden fresh carrots, dig from ground, wash well, dry overnight, pack in plastic bags and store in refrigerator and enjoy all winter.
• For a quick scalloped potato, combine frozen French fries with a homemade cheese sauce and bake until bubbly.
• Eating large cucumbers will cause chickens to produce eggs larger in size and amount.
• For the fluffiest mashed potatoes, use only russets and be careful not to overbeat. Cook just until tender; immediately drain and let stand uncovered for 1 to 2 minutes. While beating, slowly add warm milk. Do not add butter.

## MISCELLANEOUS

**Syrup:** For each cup of light syrup in a recipe, substitute one cup of sugar and 1/4 cup water. For each cup of dark corn syrup, substitute 1 cup packed brown sugar and 1/4 cup water.

**Treat for sauerkraut:** To have a tangy combination add a can of whole-berry cranberry sauce to your package of sauerkraut as it's heating plus a little brown sugar. A real treat!

**Frozen concentrate:** To use frozen concentrate to prepare juice quickly, slide it into a pitcher, add some water and mash with a potato masher. Will be a lot quicker and dissolves readily.

**Grated lemon peel:** The quickest way to make grated lemon peel for recipes is to slice off big pieces of peel and grind them for just a few seconds in a food processor.

**Hot chocolate:** To prevent "skin" from forming on top of hot chocolate beverages, beat hot cocoa with whisk until foamy.

**Stringing popcorn:** If you plan to string popcorn, pop the popcorn a few days ahead. The kernels will not break as bad when needle is pushed through.

**Ice water:** Fill a clean plastic milk jug half full of water and freeze. When ice water is needed just finish filling with water and take along on a picnic, etc.

**Brown sugar:** A little brown sugar will help flavor chili.

**Meatloaf:** Put meatloaf ingredients in a bowl and mix with a potato masher to prevent a mess, especially on your hands.

**Decorative potato or macaroni salad:** For a decorative potato or macaroni salad, dissolve a little unflavored gelatin in a small amount of water and mix with the mayonnaise before adding to the salad. Spread the salad in a mold and chill. When turned out the salad will keep its shape.

**Tender pancakes or waffles:** For light and tender pancakes or waffles, separate the egg and beat the white until stiff. Stir the yolk and other liquid ingredients into the dry ingredients, then fold in the beaten egg white.

**Venison:** Cook venison in slow cooker. Add a tad of the apple pie spice and black pepper to cut the wild flavor.

**Candles:** Before having a party or decorating with candles, put candles in the freezer for a few hours. They will not drip wax then.

**Salt:** If stew is too salty, add raw cut potatoes and discard once they have cooked and absorbed the salt. Another remedy is to add a teaspoon each of cider vinegar and sugar. Or, simply add sugar.

If soup or stew is too sweet, add salt. For a main dish or vegetable, add a teaspoon of cider vinegar.

**Gravy:** To make gravy smooth, keep a jar with a mixture of equal parts of flour and cornstarch. Put 3 or 4 tablespoons of this mixture in another jar and add some water. Shake, and in a few minutes you will have a smooth paste for gravy.

To remedy greasy gravy, add a small amount of baking soda.

For quick thickener for gravies, add some instant potatoes to your gravy and it will thicken beautifully.

Pour a cup of brewed coffee around a roast or turkey as you put it in the oven. The dark savory gravy is always perfect.

Add a few teaspoons of soy sauce to gravies and stews for a great flavor and color.

**Shrinkless links:** Boil sausage links for about 8 minutes before frying and they will shrink less and not break at all. Or, you can roll them lightly in flour before frying.

**A quick way to whip cream:** A pinch of salt added to the cream before whipping strengthens the fat cells and makes them more elastic. This helps the cream stiffen much more quickly.

**Cream that will not whip:** Chill cream, bowl and beater well. Set bowl of cream into a bowl of ice water while you're whipping. Add the white of an egg. Chill and then whip. If the cream still does not stiffen, gradually whip in 3 or 4 drops of lemon juice. Cream whipped ahead of time will not separate if you add a touch of unflavored gelatin (1/4 teaspoon per cup of cream). To eliminate a lot of mess when whipping cream with an electric beater, try this: Cut 2 holes in the middle of a piece of waxed paper, then slip the stems of the beaters through the holes and attach the beaters to the machine. Simply place paper and beaters over the bowl and whip away.

**Rock-hard brown sugar:** Add a slice of soft bread to the package of brown sugar, close the bag tightly, and in a few hours the sugar will be soft again. If you need it in a hurry, simply grate the amount called for with a hand grater. Or, put brown sugar and a cup of water (do not add to the sugar, set it alongside of it) in a covered pan. Place in the oven (low heat) for a while. Or, buy liquid brown sugar.

**Caked or clogged salt:** Tightly wrap a piece of aluminum foil around the salt shaker. This will keep the dampness out of the salt. To prevent clogging, keep 5 to 10 grains of rice inside your shaker.

**No spattering or sticking:** To keep frying food from spattering, invert a metal colander over the pan, allowing steam to escape.

Always heat the frying pan before adding oil or butter. This will keep things from sticking to the pan.

Boil vinegar in a brand new frying pan to keep things from sticking to it.

**Hurry-up hamburgers:** Poke a hole in the middle of the patties while shaping them. The burgers will cook faster and the holes will disappear when done.

**Removing the corn silk:** Dampen a paper towel or terry cloth and brush downward on the cob of corn. Every strand should come off.

**Preventing boil-overs:** Add a lump of butter or a few teaspoons of cooking oil to the water. Rice, noodles or spaghetti will not boil over or stick together.

**Softening butter:** Soften butter quickly by grating it. Or heat a small pan and place it upside-down over the butter dish for several minutes. Or place in the microwave for a few seconds.

**Measuring sticky liquids:** Before measuring honey or syrup, oil the cup with cooking oil and rinse in hot water.

**Scalded milk:** Add a bit of sugar (without stirring) to milk to prevent it from scorching.

Rinse the pan with cold water before scalding milk, and it will be much easier to clean.

**Clean and deodorize your cutting board:** Bleach it clean with lemon juice. Take away strong odors like onion with baking soda. Just rub it in.

**Keep the color in beets:** If you find that your beets tend to lose color when you boil them, add a little lemon juice.

**Broiled meat drippings:** Place a piece of bread under the rack on which you are broiling meat. Not only will this absorb the dripping fat, but it will reduce the chance of the fat catching on fire.

**Tenderized meat:** Boiled meat: Add a tablespoon of vinegar to the cooking water.

Tough meat or game: Make a marinade of equal parts cooking vinegar and heated bouillon. Marinate for 2 hours.

Steak: Simply rub in a mixture of cooking vinegar and oil. Allow to stand for 2 hours.

Chicken: To stew an old hen, soak it in vinegar for several hours before cooking. It will taste like a spring chicken.

**Unpleasant cooking odors:** While cooking vegetables that give off unpleasant odors, simmer a small pan of vinegar on top of the stove. Or, add vinegar to the cooking water. To remove the odor of fish from cooking and serving implements, rinse in vinegar water.

**No-smell cabbage:** Two things to do to keep cabbage smell from filling the kitchen: don't overcook it (keep it crisp) and put half a lemon in the water when you boil it.

**A great energy saver:** When you're near the end of the baking time, turn the oven off and keep the door closed. The heat will stay the same long enough to finish baking your cake or pie and you'll save all that energy.

**Special looking pies:** Give a unique look to your pies by using pinking shears to cut the dough. Make a pinked lattice crust!

**Removing ham rind:** Before placing ham in the roasting pan, slit rind lengthwise on the underside. The rind will peel away as the ham cooks, and can be easily removed.

**Unmolding gelatin:** Rinse the mold pan in cold water and coat with salad oil. The oil will give the gelatin a nice luster and it will easily fall out of the mold.

**No-spill cupcakes:** An ice cream scoop can be used to fill cupcake papers without spilling.

**Slicing cake or torte:** Use dental floss to slice evenly and cleanly through a cake or torte - simply stretch a length of the floss taut and press down through the cake.

**Ice cream:** Buy bulk quantities of ice cream and pack in small margarine containers. These provide individual servings.

**Canning peaches:** Don't bother to remove skins when canning or freezing peaches. They will taste better and be more nutritious with the skin on.

**How to chop garlic:** Chop in a small amount of salt to prevent pieces from sticking to the knife or chopped board. Then pulverize with the tip of the knife.

**Excess fat on soups or stews:** Remove fat from stews or soups by refrigerating and eliminating fat as it rises and hardens on the surface. Or add lettuce leaves to the pot - the fat will cling to them. Discard lettuce before serving.

**Fake sour cream:** To cut down on calories, run cottage cheese through the blender. It can be flavored with chives, extracts, etc., and used in place of mayonnaise.

**Browned butter:** Browning brings out the flavor of the butter, so only half as much is needed for seasoning vegetables if it is browned before it is added.

**Fresh garlic:** Peel garlic and store in a covered jar of vegetable oil. The garlic will stay fresh and the oil will be nicely flavored for salad dressings.

**Fluffy rice:** Rice will be fluffier and whiter if you add 1 teaspoon of lemon juice to each quart of water.

**Nutritious rice:** Cook rice in liquid saved from cooking vegetables to add flavor and nutrition. A nutty taste can be achieved by adding wheat germ to the rice.

**Jar labels:** Attach canning labels to the lids instead of the sides of jelly jars, to prevent the chore of removing the labels when the contents are gone.

**Flour puff:** Keep a powder puff in your flour container to easily dust your rolling pin or pastry board.

**Perfect noodles:** When cooking noodles, bring required amount of water to a boil, add noodles, turn heat off and allow to stand for 20 minutes. This prevents overboiling and the chore of stirring. Noodles won't stick to the pan with this method.

**Easy croutons:** Make delicious croutons for soup or salad by saving toast, cutting into cubes, and sautéing in garlic butter.

**Baked fish:** To keep fish from sticking to the pan, bake on a bed of chopped onion, celery and parsley. This also adds a nice flavor to the fish.

**Non-sticking bacon:** Roll a package of bacon into a tube before opening. This will loosen the slices and keep them from sticking together.

**Tasty hot dogs:** Boil hot dogs in sweet pickle juice and a little water for a different taste.

**Grating cheese:** Chill the cheese before grating and it will take much less time.

**Golden-brown chicken:** For golden-brown fried chicken, roll it in powdered milk instead of flour.

**Double boiler hint:** Toss a few marbles in the bottom of a double boiler. When the water boils down the noise will let you know!

**Different meatballs:** Try using crushed cornflakes or corn bread instead of bread crumbs in a meatball recipe. Or use onion-flavored potato chips.

## CLEAN-UP TIPS

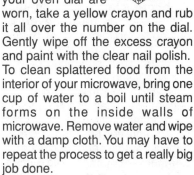

**Appliances:** To shine chrome, use vinegar or window cleaner.

If the numbers on your oven dial are worn, take a yellow crayon and rub it all over the number on the dial. Gently wipe off the excess crayon and paint with the clear nail polish.

To clean splattered food from the interior of your microwave, bring one cup of water to a boil until steam forms on the inside walls of microwave. Remove water and wipe with a damp cloth. You may have to repeat the process to get a really big job done.

To rid yellowing from white appliances try this: Mix together: 1/2 cup bleach, 1/4 cup baking soda and 4 cups warm water. Apply with a sponge and let set for 10 minutes. Rinse and dry thoroughly.

Instead of using commercial waxes, shine with rubbing alcohol.

For quick clean-ups, rub with equal parts of water and household ammonia.

Or, try club soda. It cleans and polishes at the same time.

**Blender:** Fill part way with hot water and add a drop of detergent. Cover and turn it on for a few seconds. Rinse and drain dry.

**Copper pots:** Fill a spray bottle with vinegar and add 3 tablespoons of salt. Spray solution liberally on copper pot. Let set for a while, then simply rub clean.

Dip lemon halves in salt and rub.

Or, rub with Worcestershire sauce or catsup. The tarnish will disappear. Clean with toothpaste and rinse.

**Can opener:** Loosen grime by brushing with an old toothbrush. To thoroughly clean blades, run a paper towel through the cutting process.

**Burnt and scorched pans:** Sprinkle burnt pans liberally with baking soda, adding just enough water to moisten. Let stand for several hours. You can generally lift the burned portions right out of the pan.

Stubborn stains on non-stick cookware can be removed by boiling 2 tablespoons of baking soda, 1/2 cup vinegar and 1 cup water for 10 minutes. Re-season pan with salad oil.

**Cast-iron skillets:** Clean the outside of the pan with commercial oven cleaner. Let set for 2 hours and the accumulated black stains can be removed with vinegar and water.

**Enamelware or casserole dishes:** Fill a dish that contains stuck food bits with boiling water and 2 tablespoons of baking soda. Let it stand and wash out.

**Dishes:** Save time and money by using the cheapest brand of dishwashing detergent available, but add a few tablespoons of vinegar to the dishwater. The vinegar will cut the grease and leave your dishes sparkling clean.

Before washing fine china and crystal, place a towel on the bottom of the sink to act as a cushion.

To remove coffee or tea stains and cigarette burns from fine china. Rub with a damp cloth dipped in baking soda.

**Dishwasher:** Run a cup of white vinegar through the entire cycle in an empty dishwasher to remove all soap film.

**Clogged drains:** When a drain is clogged with grease, pour a cup of salt and a cup of baking soda into the drain followed by a kettle of boiling water. The grease will usually dissolve immediately and open the drain.

Coffee grounds are a no-no. They do a nice job of clogging, especially if they get mixed with grease.

**Curtains:** To freshen curtains, throw in the dryer with a fabric softener sheet and a damp towel.

**Cobwebs:** To remove cobwebs, clean with an upward motion to lift them off. Downward motions tend to splatter them against walls.

**Dusting:** Spray furniture polish on the bristles of your broom and the dust and dirt will be easier to collect when you sweep.

**Dish Drainer:** Remove hard water stains from your dish drainer by tilting the low end of the board slightly and pouring one cup of white vinegar over the board. Let it set overnight and rub off with a sponge in the morning.

**Garbage disposal:** Grind a half lemon or orange rind in the disposal to remove any unpleasant odor.

**Glassware:** Never put a delicate glass in hot water bottom side first; it will crack from sudden expansion. The most delicate glassware will be safe if it is slipped in edgewise.

Vinegar is a must when washing crystal. Rinse in 1 part vinegar to 3 parts warm water. Air dry.

When one glass is tucked inside another, do not force them apart. Fill the top glass with cold water and dip the lower one in hot water. They will come apart without breaking.

**Grater:** For a fast and simple clean-up, rub salad oil on the grater before using.

Use a toothbrush to brush lemon rind, cheese, onion or whatever out of the grater before washing it.

**Thermos bottle:** Fill the bottle with warm water, add 1 teaspoon of baking soda and allow to soak.

**Silver:** Clean with toothbrush.

**Meat Grinder:** Before washing, run a piece of bread through it.

**Tin pie pans:** Remove rust by dipping a raw potato in cleaning powder and scouring.

**Oven:** Following a spill, sprinkle with salt immediately. When oven is cool, brush off burnt food and wipe with a damp sponge.

Sprinkle bottom of oven with automatic dishwasher soap and cover with wet paper towels. Let stand for a few hours.

A quick way to clean oven parts is to place a bath towel in the bathtub and pile all removable parts from the oven onto it. Draw enough hot water to just cover the parts and sprinkle a cup of dishwasher soap over it. While you are cleaning the inside of the oven, the rest will be cleaning itself.

An inexpensive oven cleaner: Set oven on warm for about 20 minutes, then turn off. Place a small dish of full strength ammonia on the top shelf. Put a large pan of boiling water on the bottom shelf and let it set overnight. In the morning, open oven and let it air a while before washing off with soap and water. Even the hard baked-on grease will wash off easily.

**Plastic cups, dishes and containers:** Coffee or tea stains can be scoured with baking soda.

Or, fill the stained cup with hot water and drop in a few denture cleanser tablets. Let soak for 1 hour.

To rid foul odors from plastic containers, place crumpled-up newspaper (black and white only) into the container. Cover tightly and leave overnight.

**Refrigerator:** To help eliminate odors fill a small bowl with charcoal (the kind used for potted plants) and place it on a shelf in the refrigerator. It absorbs odors rapidly.

An open box of baking soda will absorb food odors for at least a month or two.

A little vanilla poured on a piece of cotton and placed in the refrigerator will eliminate odors.

To prevent mildew from forming, wipe with vinegar. The acid effectively kills the mildew fungus.

Use a glycerine soaked cloth to wipe sides and shelves. Future spills wipe up easily. And after the freezer has been defrosted, coat the inside coils with glycerin. The next time you defrost, the ice will loosen quickly and drop off in sheets.

Wash inside and out with a mixture of 3 tablespoons of baking soda in a quart of warm water.

**Sinks:** For a sparkling white sink, place paper towels across the bottom of your sink and saturate with household bleach. Let set for 1/2 hour or so.

Rub stainless steel sinks with lighter fluid if rust marks appear. After the rust disappears wipe with your regular kitchen cleanser.

Use a cloth dampened with rubbing alcohol to remove water spots from stainless steel.

Spots on stainless steel can also be removed with white vinegar.

Club soda will shine up stainless steel sinks in a jiffy.

**Teakettle:** To remove lime deposits, fill with equal parts of vinegar and water. Bring to a boil and allow to stand overnight.

**To unplug sink:** Pour in one cup or more of white vinegar and a cup of baking soda, then add hot water out of the tap at full force. When bubbling stops, drain should be clear. Need no plumber.

**Fingerprints off the kitchen door and walls:** Take away fingerprints and grime with a solution of half water and half ammonia. Put in a spray bottle from one of these expensive cleaning products, you'll never have to buy them again.

**Formica tops:** Polish them to a sparkle with club soda.

# WINDOWS

**Window cleaning:** Newspaper is much cheaper to use for drying freshly-washed windows than paper toweling.

**Drying windows:** Dry the inside panes with up-and-down strokes, and the outside with back-and-forth motions to see which side has smudges.

**Window cleaning solution:** The best mixture for cleaning windows is 1/2 cup of ammonia, 1 cup of white vinegar and 2 tablespoons of cornstarch in a bucket of warm water.

**Cold weather window cleaning:** Add 1/2 cup of rubbing alcohol to the above mixture on cold days to prevent ice from forming on your windows.

**Clean window sills:** To remove spots on window sills, rub the surface with rubbing alcohol.

**Aluminum window frames:** Use cream silver polish to clean aluminum window frames.

**Grease spots:** Any cola drink will remove grease spots from windows.

**Numbered windows:** When cleaning, painting or changing windows, number each with a ballpoint pen and put the corresponding number inside the proper window frame.

**Window shade tears:** Repair with colorless nail polish. This works wonders on small tears.

**Cleaning screens:** For a thorough job, brush on both sides with kerosene. Wipe with a clean cloth. This method will also prevent rust from forming. Be sure to dust the screens with a small paintbrush before you begin.

For small jobs, rub a brush-type hair roller lightly over the screen and see how easily it picks up all the lint and dust.

# FURNITURE

**To remove polish build-up:** Mix 1/2 cup vinegar and 1/2 cup water. Rub with a soft cloth that has been moistened with solution, but wrung out. Dry immediately with another soft cloth.

**Polishing carved furniture:** Dip an old soft toothbrush into furniture polish and brush lightly.

**Cigarette burns:** For small minor burns, try rubbing mayonnaise into the burn. Let set for a while before wiping off with a soft cloth.

Burns can be repaired with a wax stick (available in all colors at paint and hardware stores). Gently scrape away the charred finish. Heat a knife blade and melt the shellac stick against the heated blade. Smooth over damaged area with your finger. But always consider the value of the furniture. It might be better to have a professional make the repair.

Or, make a paste of rottenstone (available at hardware stores) and salad oil. Rub into the burned spot only, following the grain of wood. Wipe clean with a cloth that has been dampened in oil. Wipe dry and apply your favorite furniture polish.

**Removing paper that is stuck to a wood surface:** Do not scrape with a knife. Pour any salad oil, a few drops at a time, on the paper. Let set for a while and rub with a soft cloth. Repeat the procedure until the paper is completely gone.

Old decals can be removed easily by painting them with several coats of white vinegar. Give the vinegar time to soak in, then gently scrape off.

**Scratches:** Make sure you always rub with the grain of the wood when repairing a scratch. Walnut: Remove the meat from a fresh, unsalted walnut or pecan nut. Break it in half and rub the scratch with the broken side of the nut.

Mahogany: You can either rub the scratch with a dark brown crayon or buff with brown paste wax.

Red Mahogany: Apply ordinary iodine with a number O artist's brush.

Maple: Combine equal amounts of iodine and denatured alcohol. Apply with a Q-tip, then dry, wax and buff.

Ebony: Use black shoe polish, black eyebrow pencil or black crayon.

Teakwood: Rub very gently with 0000 steel wool. Rub in equal amounts of linseed oil and turpentine.

Light-finished furniture: Scratches can be hidden by using tan shoe polish. However, only on shiny finishes.

For all minor scratches: Cover each scratch with a generous amount of white petroleum jelly. Allow it to remain on for 24 hours. Rub into wood. Remove excess and polish as usual.

For larger scratchers: Fill by rubbing with a wax stick (available in all colors at your hardware or paint store) or a crayon that matches the finish of the wood.

**Three solutions to remove white water rings and spots:** Dampen a soft cloth with water and put a dab of toothpaste on it. For stubborn stains, add baking soda to the toothpaste.

Make a paste of butter or mayonnaise and cigarette ashes. Apply to spot and buff away.

Apply a paste of salad oil and salt. Let stand briefly. Wipe and polish.

**Marble table-top stains:** Sprinkle salt on a fresh-cut lemon. Rub very lightly over stain. Do not rub hard or you will ruin the polished surface. Wash off with soap and water.

Scour with a water and baking soda paste. Let stand for a few minutes before rinsing with warm water.

**Removing candle wax from wooden finishes:** Soften the wax with a hair dryer. Remove wax with paper toweling and wash down with a solution of vinegar and water.

**Plastic table tops:** You will find that a coat of Turtle Wax is a quick pick-up for dulled plastic table tops and counters.

Or, rub in toothpaste and buff.

**Glass table tops:** Rub in a little lemon juice. Dry with paper towels and shine with newspaper for a sparkling table.

Toothpaste will remove small scratches from glass.

**Chrome cleaning:** For sparkling clean chrome without streaks, use a cloth dampened in ammonia.

**Removing glue:** Cement glue can be removed by rubbing with cold cream, peanut butter or salad oil.

**Wicker:** Wicker needs moisture, so use a humidifier in the winter.

To prevent drying out, apply lemon oil occasionally.

Never let wicker freeze. This will cause cracking and splitting.

Wash with a solution of warm salt water to keep from turning yellow.

**Metal furniture:** To remove rust, a good scrubbing with turpentine should accomplish this job.

**Vinyl upholstery:** Never oil vinyl as this will make it hard. It is almost impossible to soften again. For proper cleaning, sprinkle baking soda or vinegar on a rough, damp cloth, then wash with a mild dishwashing soap.

**Soiled upholstery:** Rub soiled cotton upholstery fabric with an artgum eraser or squares (purchased at stationery store).

**Leather upholstery:** Prevent leather from cracking by polishing regularly with a cream made of 1 part vinegar and 2 parts linseed oil. Clean with a damp cloth and saddle soap.

**Grease stains:** Absorb grease on furniture by pouring salt on the spill immediately.

## LAUNDRY

**Spot removal:** Two parts water and one part rubbing alcohol are the basic ingredients in any commercial spot remover.

**Clean machine:** Fill your washer with warm water and add a gallon of distilled vinegar. Run the machine through the entire cycle to unclog and clean soap scum from hoses.

**Too sudsy:** When your washer overflows with too many suds, sprinkle salt in the water - the suds will disappear.

**Hand-washed sweaters:** Add a capful of hair cream rinse to the final rinse water when washing sweaters.

**Whiter fabric:** Linen or cotton can be whitened by boiling in a mixture or 1 part cream of tartar and 3 parts water.

**Whitest socks:** Boil socks in water to which a lemon slice has been added.

**Freshen feather pillows:** Put feather pillows in the dryer and tumble, then air outside.

**Lintless corduroy:** While corduroy is still damp, brush with clothes brush to remove all lint.

**Ironing tip:** When pressing pants, iron the top part on the wrong side. Iron the legs on the right side. This gives the pockets and waistband a smooth look.

**Creaseless garments:** Take an empty cardboard paper towel roll and cut through it lengthwise. Slip it over a wire hanger to prevent a crease from forming in the garment to be hung on the hanger.

**Remove creases from hems:** Sponge material with a white vinegar solution and press flat to remove creases in hems.

**Bedroom ironing:** A good place to iron is in the bedroom. Closets are nearby to hang clothes up immediately, and the bed makes a good surface on which to fold clothes and separate items into piles.

**Ironing board cover:** When washing your ironing board cover, attach it to the board while it is still damp. When it dries, the surface will be completely smooth.

Starch your ironing board cover. This helps the cover stay clean longer.

**Lint remover:** Add a yard of nylon netting to your dryer with the wet clothes - it will catch most of the lint.

**Washer advice:** Button all buttons on clothing and turn inside out before putting into the washer. Fewer buttons will fall off and garments will fade less if turned inside out.

**Soiled collars:** Use a small paintbrush and brush hair shampoo into soiled shirt collars before laundering. Shampoo is made to dissolve body oils.

**Faster ironing:** Place a strip of heavy-duty aluminum foil over the entire length of the ironing board and cover with pad. As you iron, heat will reflect through the underside of the garment.

**Ironing embroidery:** Lay the embroidery piece upside-down on a Turkish towel before ironing. All the little spaces between the embroidery will be smooth when you are finished.

## BATHROOM

**Bathroom tile:** Rub ordinary car wax into your ceramic bathroom tiling to clean and refinish. Let it stand 10 minutes and buff or polish.

Use a typewriter eraser to clean spaces between bathroom tiles.

### Ceramic tiles

Before cleaning bathroom tiles, run the shower on *Hot* for 5 minutes to steam the dirt loose.

**Metal shower head:** To clean mineral deposits from a clogged shower head, boil it with half a cup of white vinegar.

**Plastic shower head:** Soak a plastic shower head in a hot vinegar and water mixture to unclog it.

**Shower curtains:** Before hanging shower curtains, soak them in a salt water solution to prevent mildew.

To remove mildew on shower curtains, wash them in hot soapy water, rub with lemon juice, and let them dry in the sun.

**Bathroom fixtures:** Dip a cloth in kerosene or rubbing alcohol to remove scum from your bathroom fixtures.

**Removing film and scum:** Use a piece of very fine steel wool to remove film from the shower stall.

**Porcelain cleaners:** Lighter fluid will remove most dark, stubborn stains from sink and bathtub.

**Easy bathroom cleaning:** Clean your bathroom after a steamy bath or shower. The walls, fixtures, etc., will be much easier to clean because the steam will have loosened the dirt.

**Yellowed bathtub:** Restore whiteness to a yellowed bathtub by rubbing with a salt and turpentine solution.

**Toilet:** Sometimes moisture accumulates around the toilet, leaving puddles on the floor. Prevent the condensation by applying a coat of floor wax to the tank.

**Rust stains:** Spread a paste of hydrogen peroxide and cream of tartar over the area, and add a few drops of ammonia. Let it stand for 2 or 3 hours.

**Medicine cabinet:** It's a good idea to go through your medicine cabinet several times a year and throw away medicines that are old or outdated. They could be dangerous.

**Cleaning shower doors:** Rub glass shower doors with a white vinegar-dampened sponge to remove soap residue.

**Steam-free mirror:** If your medicine cabinet has two sliding mirrors, slide one side open before taking a bath or shower. After the bath, you'll have one clean mirror instead of two that are steamed and foggy.

**Steamy bathrooms:** If you run about an inch of cold water before adding hot water to your bath, there will be absolutely no steam in your bathroom.

**Rusty tile:** Rust stains on tile can be removed with kerosene.

**Sink cleaners:** Light stains can often be removed by simply rubbing with a cut lemon.

For dark stains, and especially rust, rub with a paste of borax and lemon juice.

**Sweet-smelling bathroom:** Place a fabric softener sheet in the wastepaper basket. Or, add a touch of fragrance by dabbing your favorite perfume on a light bulb. When the light is on, the heat releases the aroma.

## HANDY PERSON

**Rule to remember:** Left is loose and right is tight.

**Plywood cutting:** Put a strip of masking tape at the point of plywood where you plan to begin sawing to keep it from splitting.

**Locating wall studs:** Move a pocket compass along the wall. When the needle moves, usually the stud will be located at that point. Studs are usually located 16" apart.

**Fraying rope:** Shellac the ends of the rope to prevent fraying.

Heat the cut end of the nylon cord over a match flame to bond the end together.

**Loosening rusty bolts:** Apply a cloth soaked in any carbonated soda to loosen rusted bolts.

**Sandpaper hint:** By dampening the backing on sandpaper, it will last longer and resist cracking.

**Tight screws:** Loosen a screw by putting a couple of drops of peroxide on it and letting it soak in.

**Loose drawer knobs:** Before inserting a screw into the knob, coat with fingernail polish to hold it tightly.

**Screwdriver tip:** Keep a screwdriver tip from slipping by putting chalk on the blade.

**Loosening joints:** Loosen old glue by applying vinegar from an oil can to the joint.

**Sticking drawers:** Rub the runners of drawers with a candle or a bar of soap so they will slide easily.

**Stubborn locks:** Dip key into machine oil or graphite to loosen up a lock.

**Slamming doors:** Reduce the noise level in your home by putting self-sticking protective pads on the inside edges of cabinet doors, cupboards, etc.

**Icy sidewalk tip:** Sprinkle sand through a strainer on an icy sidewalk to distribute evenly.

**Garbage can tip:** Garbage cans will last longer if they are painted. Use primer on galvanized metal, then paint with matching house paint.

**Towel rack tip:** Replace the bottom screws of towel racks with cup hooks. Small towels and washcloths may be hung from them.

**Screen repair:** Use clear cement glue to repair a small hole in wire screening.

**Hairdryer hint:** Thaw a frozen pipe with a portable hairdryer.

**Finding a gas leak:** Lather the pipes with soapy water. The escaping gas will cause the soapy water to bubble, revealing the damaged areas. You can make a temporary plug by moistening a cake of soap and pressing it over the spot. When the soap hardens, it will effectively close the leak until the gasman comes.

**Hanging pictures:** Before you drive nails into the wall, mark the spot with an X of cellophane tape. This trick will keep the plaster from cracking when you start hammering.

When the landlady says, "no nails in the wall", hang pictures with sewing machine needles. They will hold up to 30 pounds.

## BEAUTY

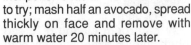

**Natural facial:** A good and inexpensive facial to try; mash half an avocado, spread thickly on face and remove with warm water 20 minutes later.

**Your own manicure:** Soak your hands in warm water with lemon juice added. Take them out after about 8 minutes. Rub some lemon peel over the nails while you gently push back the cuticle. Then buff with a soft cloth.

**Baking soda for teeth:** Baking soda instead of toothpaste does as good a job. It also works on dentures.

**Sunburn relief:** A wonderful relief for sunburn pain is the application of mint-flavored milk of magnesia to the skin.

Dab on some apple cider vinegar. The pinkness and pain will disappear.

For a super bad burn, put on a paste of water and baking soda.

**Hair shiner:** These hair rinses will remove soap film and shine hair: For blondes, rinse water containing a few tablespoons of lemon juice. For brunettes and redheads, a few tablespoons of apple cider vinegar in the rinse water.

**Broken lipstick:** Hold a match under the broken ends until they melt enough to adhere to each other. Cool in the refrigerator.

**Nail polish:** Don't throw away that gummy nail polish. Place the bottle in boiling water to bring it back to its original consistency.

Instead of storing the nail polish bottle right-side-up, put it on its side. Stir it up with the brush when you need some.

Before you put on polish, put vinegar on your nails. It will clean them completely and help nail polish stick longer.

**Cleaning combs and brushes:** A solution of baking soda and hot water cleans hair brushes and combs.

**Hair conditioner:** Mayonnaise gives dry hair a good conditioning. Apply 1/2 cup mayonnaise to dry, unwashed hair. Cover with plastic bag and wait for 15 minutes. Rinse a few times before shampooing thoroughly.

**Tired eyes:** Place fresh cold cucumbers slices on your eyelids to rid them of redness and puffiness.

**Dry skin:** The best remedy is also the easiest to find: water. Drink six to eight glasses a day and eat foods high in water content, such as fruits and leafy vegetables. Use a humidifier in winter.

Bathe in mildly salted water (1/2 cup of salt per bath) to rehydrate your body, then apply a cream or lotion that will act as a moisturizer.

For an easy facial, mash a banana, add a tablespoon of honey and smooth the mixture on your face. After 15 minutes, rinse with warm water.

**Oily skin:** To help normalize skin, avoid spicy foods, reduce oils and fats in your diet and drink six to eight glasses of water daily.

For a refreshing facial, fill a spray bottle with tepid water and 1 teaspoon of salt, then spray the solution on your face. Blot dry with a towel. For a quick steam, heat a wet towel in the microwave and form a tent over your face.

Here's a quick facial mask: Mix 3 tablespoons each of mineral water and Fuller's Earth and apply the paste to your face. After 20 minutes rinse with warm water. Or try a paste of warm water and oatmeal for 10 minutes.

**Pimples:** Here's some single-pimple camouflage: use a little green eye shadow to neutralize the redness, then cover with foundation.

**Puffiness:** If your hands are puffy, hold them over your head for a couple of minutes; repeat at least three or four times a day. Elevate swollen feet for a minimum of 15 minutes.

## SEWING

**Threading needles:** Apply some hair spray to your finger and to the end of the thread, stiffening it enough to be easily threaded.

**Sharp machine needles:** Sharpen sewing machine needles by stitching through sandpaper.

**Buttons:** Coat the center of buttons with clear nail polish and they'll stay on longer.

On a four-hole button, sew through two holes at a time, knotting the thread and tying off for each set of holes.

Use dental floss or elastic thread to sew buttons on children's clothing. The buttons will take a lot of wear before falling off.

**Dropped needles and pins:** Instead of groping around your floor for fallen needles and pins, keep a magnet in your sewing kit, simply sweep it across your rug to pick up those strays.

**Sewing machine oil:** Stitch through a blotter after oiling your sewing machine to prevent extra oil from damaging your garments.

**Patterns:** Instead of trying to fit used patterns back into their envelopes, store them in plastic bags.

Keep patterns from tearing and wrinklefree by spraying with spray starch.

**Heavy seams:** Rub seams with a bar of soap to allow a sewing machine needle to easily pass through.

**Sewing on nylon:** When repairing seams on nylon jackets or lingerie, make the job a lot simpler by placing a piece of paper underneath the section you are going to sew. Stitch through the fabric and paper. When finished, tear the paper off.

## FOOD STORAGE

**Baking Powder:** Store the airtight tins in a cool, dry place and replace every 6 months.

**Baking Soda:** Store in an airtight container in a cool, dry place for about 6 months.

**Beans:** Once a package is opened, dry beans should not be refrigerated but stored in airtight containers in a cold, dry place. They will keep for about 1 year.

**Bread:** A rib of celery in your bread bag will keep the bread fresh for a longer time.

**Brown Sugar:** Wrap in a plastic bag and store in a tightly covered container for up to 4 months.

**Cakes:** Putting half an apple in the cake box will keep cake moist.

**Celery and lettuce:** Store in refrigerator in paper bags instead of plastic. Leave the outside leaves and stalks on until ready to use.

**Cheese:** Wrap cheese in a vinegar-dampened cloth to keep it from drying out.

**Chocolate:** Store chocolate for no longer than 1 year. It should be kept in a cool, dry place with a temperature range of 60°F to 75°F. If the storage temperature exceeds 75°F, some of the cocoa butter may separate and rise to the surface, causing a whitish color to the chocolate called "bloom".

**Cocoa:** Store cocoa in a glass jar in a dry and cool place.

**Cookies:** Place crushed tissue paper on the bottom of your cookie jar.

**Cottage Cheese:** Store carton upside-down. It will keep twice as long.

**Dried Fruit:** Store unopened packages of dried fruit in a cool, dry place or in the refrigerator. Store opened packages in an airtight container in the refrigerator or freezer for 6 to 8 months.

**Flour:** Store flour in a clean, tightly covered container for up to 1 year at room temperature.

**Garlic:** Garlic should be stored in a dry, airy place away from light. Garlic cloves can be kept in the freezer.

When ready to use, peel and chop before thawing. Or, garlic cloves will never dry out if you store them in a bottle of cooking oil. After the garlic is used up, you can use the garlic flavored oil for salad dressing.

**Granulated Sugar:** Store sugar in a tightly covered container for up to 2 years.

**Honey:** Put honey in small plastic freezer containers to prevent sugaring. It also thaws out in a short time.

**Ice Cream:** Ice cream that has been opened and returned to the freezer sometimes forms a waxlike film on the top. To prevent this, after part of the ice cream has been removed press a piece of waxed paper against the surface and reseal the carton.

**Lemons:** Store whole lemons in a tightly sealed jar of water in the refrigerator. They will yield much more juice than when first purchased.

**Limes:** Store limes, wrapped in tissue paper, on lower shelf of the refrigerator.

**Marshmallows:** They will not dry out if stored in the freezer. Simply cut with scissors when ready to use.

**Nuts:** For optimum freshness and shelf life, nuts should be stored, preferably unshelled, in a tightly covered container in the refrigerator or freezer and shelled as needed. (The shell and the cool temperature keep the nut from turning rancid.)

**Olive Oil:** You can lengthen the life of olive oil by adding a cube of sugar to the bottle.

**Onions:** Wrap individually in foil to keep them from becoming soft or sprouting. Once an onion has been cut in half, rub the leftover side with butter and it will keep fresh longer.

**Parsley:** Keep fresh and crisp by storing in a wide-mouth jar with a tight lid. Parsley may also be frozen.

**Popcorn:** It should always be kept in the freezer. Not only will it stay fresh, but freezing helps eliminate "old-maids".

**Potatoes:** Potatoes, as well as other root vegetables, keep well in a dark, cool place, preferably a cellar. Store them in a dark brown paper bag.

**Shredded Coconut:** Store in a cool, dry place in an airtight container. Do not store in the refrigerator.

**Smoked Meats:** Wrap ham or bacon in a vinegar-soaked cloth, then in waxed paper to preserve freshness.

**Soda Crackers:** Wrap tightly and store in the refrigerator.

**Strawberries:** Keep in a colander in the refrigerator. Wash just before serving.

**Vegetables with tops:** Remove the tops on carrots, beets, etc. before storing.

**Yeast:** Store in the freezer or refrigerator in a closed plastic bag.

## MEAT

**Beef**

| | |
|---|---|
| Roasts | 3 to 5 days |
| Steaks | 3 to 5 days |
| Ground beef, stew meat | 2 days |

**Pork**

| | |
|---|---|
| Roasts | 3 to 5 days |
| Hams, picnics, whole | 7 days |
| Bacon | 7 to 14 days |
| Chops, spareribs | 2 to 3 days |
| Pork sausage | 1 to 2 days |

**Veal**

| | |
|---|---|
| Roasts | 3 to 5 days |
| Chops | 4 days |

**Lamb**

| | |
|---|---|
| Roasts | 3 to 5 days |
| Chops | 3 to 5 days |
| Ground lamb | 2 days |

**Poultry**

| | |
|---|---|
| Chickens, whole | 1 to 2 days |
| Chickens, cut up | 2 days |
| Turkeys, whole | 1 to 2 days |

**Cooked meats**

Leftover cooked meats . 4 days
Cooked poultry .............. 2 days
Hams, picnics ................ 7 days
Frankfurters .................. 4 to 5 days
Sliced luncheon meats . 3 days
Unsliced bologna .......... 4 to 6 days

## TO REMOVE STAINS FROM WASHABLES

**Alcoholic beverages:** Pre-soak or sponge fresh stains immediately with cold water, then with cold water and glycerin. Rinse with vinegar for a few seconds if stain remains. These stains may turn brown with age. If wine stain remains, rub with concentrated detergent; wait 15 minutes; rinse. Repeat if necessary. Wash with detergent in hottest water safe for fabric.

**Baby Food:** Use liquid laundry detergent and brush into stain with an old toothbrush then wash.

**Blood:** Pre-soak in cold or warm water at least 30 minutes. If stain remains, soak in lukewarm ammonia water (3 tablespoons per gallon water). Rinse. If stain remains, work in detergent, and wash, using bleach safe for fabric.

**Candle wax:** Use a dull knife to scrape off as much as possible. Place fabric between 2 blotters or facial tissues and press with warm iron. Remove color stain with non-flammable dry cleaning solvent. Wash with detergent in the hottest water safe for fabric.

**Chewing gum:** Rub area with ice, then scrape off with a dull blade. Sponge with dry cleaning solvent; allow to air dry. Wash in detergent and hottest water safe for fabric.

**Chocolate and cocoa:** Sponge with club soda.

**Coffee:** Sponge or soak with cold water as soon as possible. Wash, using detergent and bleach safe for fabric. Remove cream grease stains with non-flammable dry cleaning solvent. Wash again.

**Cosmetics:** Loosen stain with a non-flammable dry cleaning solvent. Rub detergent in until stain outline is gone. Wash in hottest water and detergent safe for fabric.

**Crayon:** Scrape with dull blade. Place item between paper towels, press with warm iron. Repeat, only with new paper towels. Wash in hottest water safe for fabric, with detergent and 1 to 2 cups of baking soda. NOTE: If full load is crayon stained, take to cleaners or coin-op dry cleaning machines.

**Deodorants:** Sponge area with white vinegar. If stain remains, soak with denatured alcohol. Wash with detergent in hottest water safe for fabric.

**Dye:** If dye transfers from a non-colorfast item during washing, immediately bleach discolored items. Repeat as necessary BEFORE drying. On whites use color remover. CAUTION: Do not use color remover in washer, or around washer and dryer as it may damage the finish.

**Egg:** Scrape with dull blade. Pre-soak in cold or warm water for at least 30 minutes. Remove grease with dry cleaning solvent. Wash in hottest water safe for fabric, with detergent.

**Fruit and fruit juices:** Sponge with cold water. Pre-soak in cold or warm water for at least 30 minutes. Wash with detergent and bleach safe for fabric.

**Grass:** Pre-soak in cold water for at least 30 minutes. Rinse. Pre-treat with detergent, hot water, and bleach safe for fabric. On acetate and colored fabrics, use 1 part of alcohol to 2 parts water.

**Grease, oil, tar or butter:** Method 1: Use powder or chalk absorbents to remove as much grease as possible. Pre-treat with detergent or non-flammable dry cleaning solvent, or liquid shampoo. Wash in hottest water safe for fabric, using plenty of detergent.
Method 2: Rub spot with lard and sponge with a non-flammable dry cleaning solvent. Wash in hottest water and detergent safe for fabric.
**Ink-ball-point pen:** Spray with hair spray and launder.
**Ketchup or Mustard:** Scrape excess. Use commercial spot remover. Rinse; launder.
**Liquor:** Sponge stain with cool water. Soak in solution of cool water and dishwashing liquid: 30 minutes for light-stain, overnight for heavy. Rinse; launder.
**Meat Juices:** Scrape with dull blade. Pre-soak in cold or warm water for 30 minutes. Wash with detergent and bleach safe for fabric.
**Mildew:** Pre-treat as soon as possible with detergent. Wash. If any stain remains, sponge with lemon juice and salt. Dry in sun. Wash, using hottest water, detergent and bleach safe for fabric. NOTE: Mildew is very hard to remove; treat promptly.
**Milk, cream, ice cream:** Pre-soak in cold or warm water for 30 minutes. Wash. Sponge any grease spots with non-flammable dry cleaning solvent. Wash again.
**Mud:** Let stain dry. Brush off; launder. Tough stain: Soak in cool water for 30 minutes; work liquid laundry detergent into stain; rinse.
**Nail polish:** Sponge with acetone-based polish remover or banana oil. Wash. If stain remains, sponge with denatured alcohol to which a few drops of ammonia have been added. Wash again. Do not use polish remover on acetate or triacetate fabrics.
**Paint:** Oil base: Sponge stains with turpentine, cleaning fluid or paint remover. Pre-treat and wash in hot water. For old stains, sponge with banana oil and then with non-flammable dry cleaning solvent. Wash again.
Water base: Scrape off paint with dull blade. Wash with detergent in water as hot as is safe for fabric.
**Perspiration:** Sponge fresh stain with ammonia; old stain with vinegar. Pre-soak in cold or warm water. Rinse. Wash in hottest water safe for fabric. If fabric is yellowed, use bleach. If stain still remains, dampen and sprinkle with meat tenderizer, or pepsin. Let stand 1 hour. Brush off and wash. For persistent odor, sponge with colorless mouthwash.
**Rust:** Soak in lemon juice and salt or oxalic acid solution (3 tablespoons oxalic acid to 1 pint warm water). A commercial rust remover may be used. CAUTION: HANDLE POISONOUS RUST REMOVERS CAREFULLY. KEEP OUT OF REACH OF CHILDREN. NEVER USE OXALIC ACID OR ANY RUST REMOVER AROUND WASHER OR DRYER AS IT CAN DAMAGE THE FINISH. SUCH CHEMICALS MAY ALSO REMOVE PERMANENT PRESS FABRIC FINISHES.
**Scorch:** Wash with detergent and bleach safe for fabric. On heavier scorching, cover stain with cloth dampened with hydrogen peroxide. Cover this with dry cloth and press with hot iron. Rinse well. CAUTION: Severe scorching cannot be removed because of fabric damage.
**Soft drinks:** Sponge immediately with cold water and alcohol. Heat and detergent may set stain.
**Tea:** Sponge or soak with cold water as soon as possible. Wash using detergent and bleach safe for fabric.

## STAINS ON CARPETS AND FLOORS

**Flatten shag carpets:** Raise flattened spots in your carpet where heavy furniture has stood by using a steam iron. Hold the iron over the spot and build up a good steam. Then brush up the carpet.

**Candle drippings:** For spilled wax on carpet, use a brown paper bag as a blotter and run a hot iron over it, which will absorb the wax.

**Dog stains:** Blot up excess moisture with paper towel. Pour club soda on the spot and continue blotting. Lay a towel over the spot and set a heavy object on top in order to absorb all the moisture.

**Rug care:** When washing and drying foam-backed throw rugs, never wash in hot water, and use the "air only" dryer setting to dry. Heat will ruin foam.

**Cleaning rugs:** If the rug is only slightly dirty, you can clean it with cornmeal. Use a stiff brush to work the cornmeal into the pile of the rug. Take it all out with the vacuum.

**Spills on the rug:** When spills happen, go to the bathroom and grab a can of shaving cream. Squirt it on the spot then rinse off with water.

**Ballpoint ink marks:** Saturate the spots with hairspray. Allow to dry. Brush lightly with a solution of water and vinegar.

**Glue:** Glue can be loosened by saturating the spot with a cloth soaked in vinegar.

**Repairing braided rugs:** Braided rugs often rip apart. Instead of sewing them, use clear fabric glue to repair. It's that fast and easy.

**Repairing a burn:** Remove some fuzz from the carpet, either by shaving or pulling out with a tweezer. Roll into the shape of the burn. Apply a good cement glue to the backing of the rug and press the fuzz down into the burned spot. Cover with a piece of cleansing tissue and place a heavy book on top. This will cause the glue to dry very slowly and will get the best results.

**Spot remover for outdoor carpeting:** Spray spots liberally with a pre-wash commercial spray. Let it set several minutes, then hose down and watch the spots disappear.

**Blood on the rug:** When you get blood on your rug, rub off as much as you can at first, then take a cloth soaked in cold water and wet the spot, wiping it up as you go. If a little bit remains, pour some ammonia onto the cool, wet cloth and lightly wipe that over the spot, too. Rinse it right away with cold water.

**Crayon Marks:** Use silver polish to remove from vinyl tile or linoleum.

**Spilled nail polish:** Allow to almost dry, then peel off of waxed floors or tile.

**Tar spots:** Use paste wax to remove tar from floors. Works on shoes, too.

**Dusting floors:** Stretch a nylon stocking over the dust mop. After using, discard the stocking and you will have a clean mop.

**Varnished floors:** Use cold tea to clean woodwork and varnished floors.

**Spilled grease:** Rub floor with ice cubes to solidify grease. Scrape up excess and wash with soapy water.

**Quick shine:** Put a piece of waxed paper under your dust mop. Dirt will stick to the mop and the wax will shine your floors.

**Unmarred floors:** Put thick old socks over the legs of heavy furniture when moving across floors.

**Wood floor care:** Never use water or water-based cleaners on wood floors. Over a period of time, warping and swelling will develop.

**Heel marks:** Just take a pencil eraser and wipe them off.

**Floor polisher:** When cleaning the felt pads of your floor polisher, place the pads between layers of newspaper and press with an iron to absorb built-up wax.

**Garage floors:** In an area where a large amount of oil has spilled, lay several thicknesses of newspaper. Saturate the paper with water; press flat against the floor. When dry, remove the newspaper and the spots will have disappeared.

**Basement floors:** Sprinkle sand on oily spots, let it absorb the oil, and sweep up.

**Fix those loose linoleum edges:** Take a knife with some tile adhesive and work it under the loose part. Put a heavy weight, such as a big stack of books, over the whole area and keep it weighed down for the amount of time it says on the can of adhesive.

## 99 WAYS YOU CAN SAVE THE EARTH

1. Buy plain white toilet paper, tissues and paper towels. Dyed paper pollutes.

2. Instead of ammonia-based cleaners, use vinegar and water or baking soda and water.

3. Walk or ride a bike instead of using the car for short trips.

4. Reuse your grocery bags, or buy a string bag you can carry your groceries in.

5. Buy eggs and milk in cardboard cartons instead of plastic. Or recycle your plastic milk jugs.

6. Take showers instead of baths to save water and energy.

7. Keep your car tires inflated to the proper pressure to improve fuel economy and extend the life of the tires.

8. Don't use electric tools and appliances when hand-operated ones will do the job.

9. Choose a light-colored car with tinted glass to lessen the need for air conditioning.

10. Use mulch and natural ground covers in gardens to contain moisture and conserve water use.

11. Instead of ironing, hang clothes in the bathroom while you shower.

12. Turn off lights in rooms you aren't using.

13. Replace incandescent bulbs with more efficient screw-in compact fluorescent bulbs or fluorescent fixtures.

14. Use high-quality multigrade oil in your car to increase fuel efficiency.

15. Air-dry laundry when possible.

16. Avoid keeping refrigerator or freezer too cold. Government recommended temperature for fresh food is 38 degrees F. For freezers it's 5 degrees F.

17. Reuse aluminum foil and plastic wrap, or avoid them completely by using plastic containers.

18. Plant trees. Strategically located, trees can reduce heating and cooling bills, help prevent soil erosion and reduce air pollution.

19. Water lawns at night to limit evaporation.

20. Compost your leaves and yard waste. You'll improve your garden's soil and avoid sending yard waste to the landfill.

21. Minimize the use of garden chemicals by weeding.

22. Be sure to return your recyclable cans and bottles for your deposit.

23. Don't pour oil and gasoline into the sewer system or on the ground. Take to your local collection site.

24. Buy rechargeable batteries.

25. Use cold water rather than hot water whenever possible for kitchen tasks and laundry.

26. Share rides to work or use public transportation.

27. Buy a fuel-efficient car. Aim for 35 miles per gallon.

28. Read labels and research the products you buy.

29. Don't use excessive amounts of detergent. Presoak dirty laundry.

30. Insulate your basement to save 1/3 on your heat bill.

31. Buy products packaged in recycled paper or cardboard.

32. Caulk and weatherstrip doors and windows.

33. Ask your utility company for an energy audit to assess energy waste in your home.

34. Install water-conserving showerheads and sink-faucet aerators.

35. Insulate your water heater. Turn it down to 121 degrees F.

36. Limit or eliminate your use of "disposable" items.

37. Close off unused areas of your home. Shut off or block heat vents.

38. Compare Energy Guide labels when buying appliances.

39. Keep the fireplace damper closed to prevent heat escape. Keep glass fireplace doors closed when a fire is burning.

40. Use an automatic setback thermostat to turn down heat when you're not home and at night.

41. Capture free solar heat in the winter by opening curtains on south windows during sunny days.

42. Clean lamps and lighting fixtures regularly.

43. Thaw frozen foods in the refrigerator to reduce cooking times and to ensure food safety.

44. Tune up your car regularly for maximum gas mileage.

45. Remove unnecessary items from your car. Each 100 pounds of weight decreases fuel efficiency by 1%.

46. Don't speed; accelerate and slow down gradually.

47. Use latex and other water-based paints instead of toxic enamel or oil-based paints.

48. Repair leaks and drips as soon as they occur. A moderate drip wastes two gallons of water or more per hour.

49. Rent or borrow items you don't often use. Efficient use of products conserves resources.

50. Use small electric pans and ovens to reduce energy use.

51. Run your dishwasher only when full, and use the energy saver cycle.

52. Avoid products made from tropical rainforest woods.

53. Request a Household Hazardous Waste Wheel, showing alternatives to hazardous products, from the Department of Natural Resources, 1-800-DNR-1025 (cost $1.25).

54. For furniture polish, use 1 part lemon juice, 2 parts olive or vegetable oil.

55. For a toilet bowl cleaner, use baking soda and a brush.

56. As a general cleaner, use 1/2 cup borax in 1 gallon water.

57. Instead of chemical air fresheners, set a cotton ball soaked in vanilla extract on a saucer. (Keep away from children and pets.)

58. Instead of toxic mothballs, use cedar chips.

59. Roach killer: mix baking soda and powdered sugar. (Keep away from children and pets.)

60. Ant killer: Use chili powder to hinder entry.

61. Do not toss toxic chemicals into your garbage. Call the Groundwater Hotline 1-800-DNR-1025 to find out how to dispose, or keep them for a Toxic Cleanup Day.

62. Use pump sprays instead of aerosols.

63. Use a holding tank on your boat and don't empty toilet tanks into the

water.

64. Don't litter. Pick up any you see, especially plastic rings that can trap birds and fish.

65. Take your own coffee cup to work instead of using disposables.

66. Pour a kettle of boiling water down the drain weekly to melt fat that may be building up.

67. Take old tires to a landfill or processing center for proper disposal.

68. Buy recycled paper, stationery and greeting cards.

69. Shop at your local farmers market. Products are fresh, packaging is minimal and foods are less likely to be made with preservatives.

70. Start an organic garden.

71. Buy in bulk to avoid over packaging.

72. Avoid optional equipment on cars that decreases fuel economy.

73. When having air conditioners serviced, choose companies that will recycle freon instead of venting it.

74. Keep lint screen in dryer clean.

75. Use a trash bag in your car instead of throwing trash out the window.

76. Consider using cloth diapers instead of disposal ones. Check for a local diaper service.

77. Urge your local community to start a curbside recycling program.

78. Start a recycling program where you work. Contact the Department of Natural Resources about the Waste Reduction Assistance Program (WRAP) at 1-800-DNR-1025.

79. Insulate your waterbed by adding an inch of polyethylene foam around the edges and the bottom.

80. To remove rust, rub rust spots briskly with a piece of crumpled aluminum foil, shiny side up.

81. Give leftover paint to theater groups, schools or church groups.

82. Call your local humane society to see if they can use your old newspapers for animal bedding.

83. Check your smoke detector. Put a new battery in if it needs one. Some detectors contain small amounts of low-level radioactive waste. Send used or broken detectors back to the manufacturer.

84. Use equal parts white vinegar and warm water to wash windows or glass. Dry with a soft cloth.

85. Install storm windows.

86. When using hazardous products, use only what is needed. Twice as much does not mean twice the results.

87. Arrange for a waste management presentation for your club or business.

88. Read publications that educate about long-term sustainability.

89. Educate your children about the environment.

90. Write a letter to the editor about your environmental concerns.

91. Get involved in a local treeplanting effort.

92. Learn about global climate change.

93. Join an environmental organization.

94. Research environmental legislation and write to your representatives in the state legislature and in Congress.

95. Think about the kind of Earth you would like to see for your grandchildren's grandchildren.

96. Plan an environmental activity for your club or troop, such as a recycling program.

97. Investigate the environmental record of companies you invest in. Write a letter as a shareholder to the company president or sell your stock.

98. Talk to friends, relatives and co-workers about the environment.

99. Copy this list and send it to your friends.

## PLANTS

• Always choose a pot that's not more than two inches larger in diameter than the old pot.

• Blooming plants should be repotted after they're done blossoming, not before.

• To help reduce the shock of repotting, give the new soil a thorough watering.

• Clay pots should be soaked in water for a few minutes before you repot your plants. This prevents the clay from absorbing moisture from the potting soil.

• Fill a string mesh bag with suet and scraps of leftover food and hang from a tree limb for those cheery winter birds.

• Take old Christmas tree outside and stabilize in the ground. Hang grapefruit and orange cups from the branches with wire and fill cups with bird seed for the birdies.

• When you start seeds indoors, it's best to plant them in a small amount of dirt at first. Gradually add more dirt as the plant grows. Do this and your plants will be much stronger and do better after you set them outside.

• If you have a large garden, but not a lot of time to weed, put two layers of newspaper between your rows. This keeps the weeds down and saves you a lot of time.

• Plant pole beans next to sunflowers. The beans will climb the lower part of the sunflowers and you won't need any poles.

• Your African Violets will bloom longer, prettier and more abundantly if you stick a few rusty nails in the soil alongside them.

• After holidays–remove branches from the Christmas tree and put them over flower beds for insulation.

Thank you for purchasing this cookbook. We hope you will enjoy it for years to come. For 30 years, G&R Publishing has produced thousands of beautiful cookbooks for clubs, schools, churches, businesses, families and civic organizations. Have you ever considered putting one together for your own group or family?

All you have to do is collect recipes from your members and send them to us. We put them in book form with your choice of cover, dividers and extras. It's as easy as that! You can add history, hints and photos to personalize your book. Every recipe contributor gets credit in the book, making the project unique

and meaningful. It's easy to be excited about something with that "personal touch".

Whether you are making money for your group or organization or making memories for your family, G & R can help you. Please call our toll free number or visit our website to receive our free information. _Fundraising Has Never Been So Easy!!_

**The Cookbook Specialists...**
**G & R**
Publishing Co.
**507 Industrial Street**
**Waverly, IA 50677**
**1-800-383-1679**
**www.cookbookprinting.com**

*To help you choose the Best Cookbook Company, take advantage of this special offer.*

- - - - - - - - - - - - - - - - - - - - - - - -

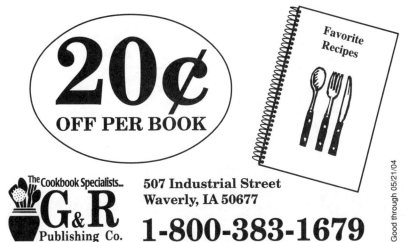